Frederic Remington:
113 Paintings and Drawings

I0474605

By Maria Tsaneva

First Edition

*****

Foreword

Frederic Sackrider Remington (1861 – 1909) was an American painter, illustrator, sculptor, and writer who specialized in depictions of the Old American West, specifically concentrating on the last quarter of the 19th-century American West and images of cowboys, American Indians, and the U. S. Cavalry.

Remington was the most successful Western illustrator in the "Golden Age" of illustration at the end of the 19th Century and the beginning of the 20th Century, so much so that the other Western artists such as Charles Russell and Charles Schreyvogel were known during Remington's life as members of the "School of Remington". His style was naturalistic, sometimes impressionistic, and usually veered away from the ethnographic realism of earlier Western artists such as George Catlin. His focus was firmly on the people and animals of the West, with landscape usually of secondary importance, unlike the members and descendants of the Hudson River School, such as Frederic Edwin Church, Albert Bierstadt, and Thomas Moran, who glorified the vastness of the West and the dominance of nature over man. He took artistic liberties in his depictions of human action, and for the sake of his readers' and publishers' interest. Though always confident in his subject matter, Remington was less sure about his colors, and critics often harped on his palette, but his lack of confidence drove him to experiment and produce a great variety of effects, some very true to nature and some imagined.

Remington was one of the first American artists to illustrate the true gait of the horse in motion (along with Thomas Eakins), as validated by the famous sequential photographs of Eadweard Muybridge. Previously, horses in full gallop were usually depicted with all four legs pointing out, like "hobby horses". The galloping horse became Remington's signature subject, copied and interpreted by many Western artists who followed him, adopting the correct anatomical motion. Though criticized by some for his use of photography, Remington often created depictions that slightly exaggerated natural motion to satisfy the eye. He wrote, "The artist must know more than the camera... (the horse must be) incorrectly drawn from the photographic standpoint (to achieve the desired effect)."

Furthermore, Remington's skill as a businessman was equal to his artistry, unlike many other artists who relied on their spouses or business agents or no one at all to run their financial affairs. He was an effective publicist and promoter of his art. He insisted that his originals be handled carefully and returned to him in pristine condition (without editor's marks) so he could sell them. He carefully regulated his output to maximize his income and kept detailed notes about his works and his sales.

Paintings and Drawings

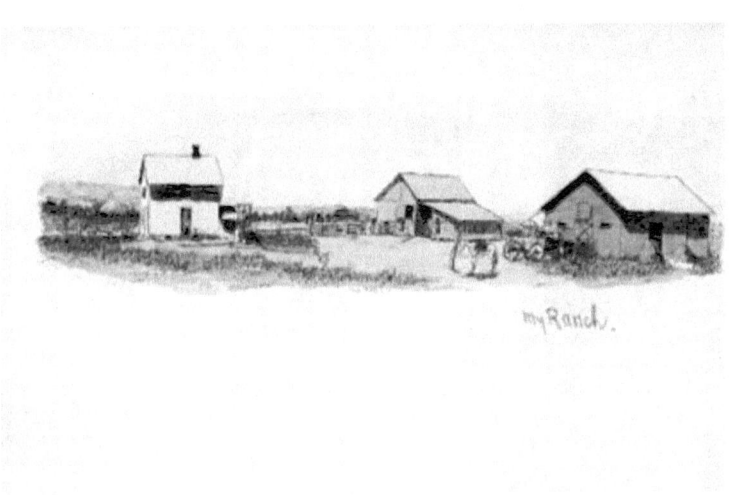

My Ranch, 1883, watercolor

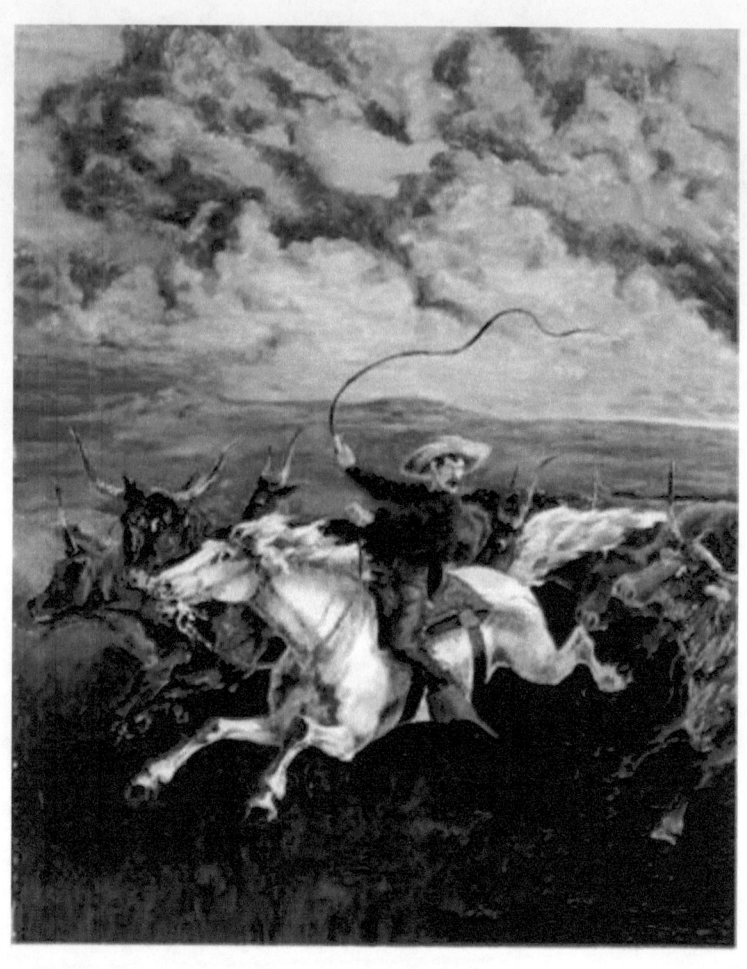

Prarie Fire, 1885, oil

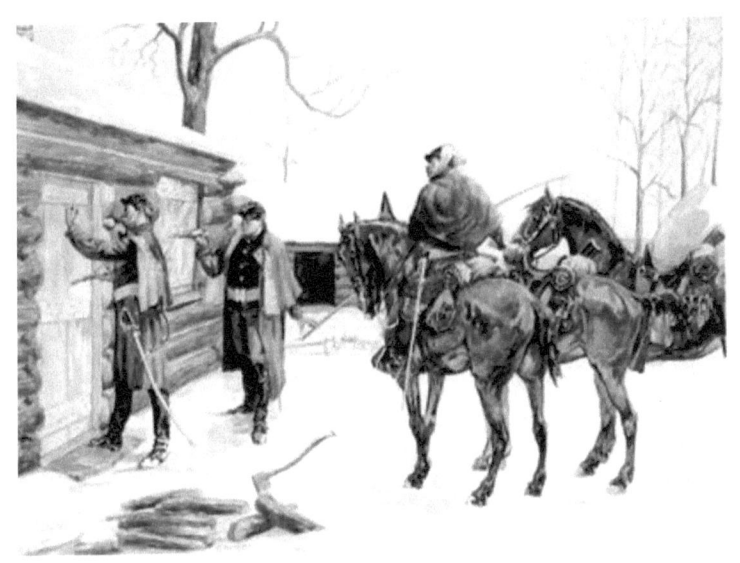

Arresting the Deserter, 1885, watercolor

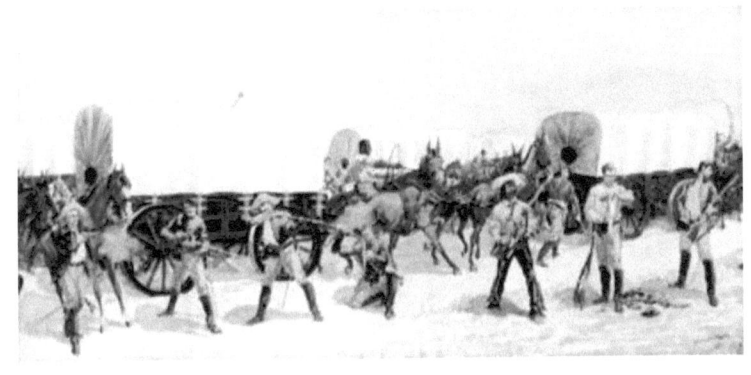

Attack on the Supply Train, 1885, watercolor

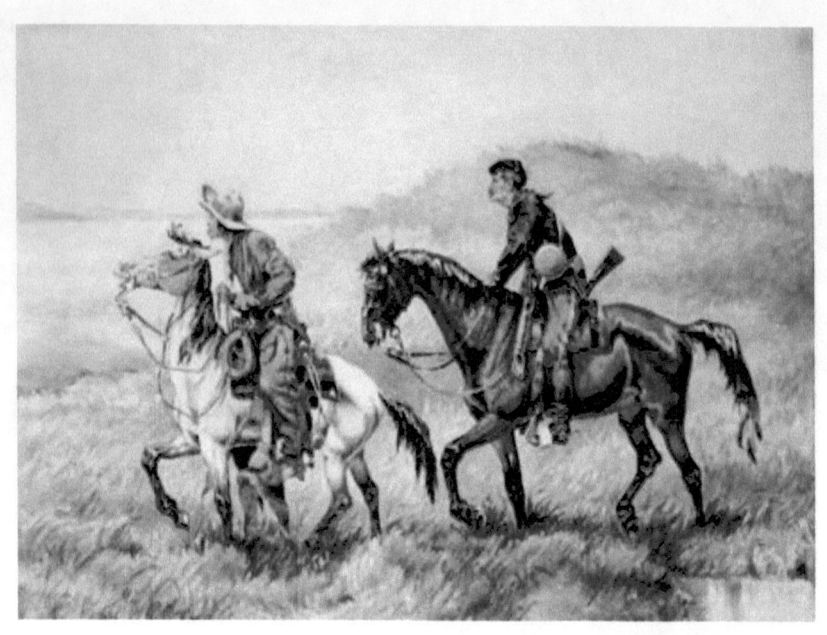

The Couriers, 1885, watercolor

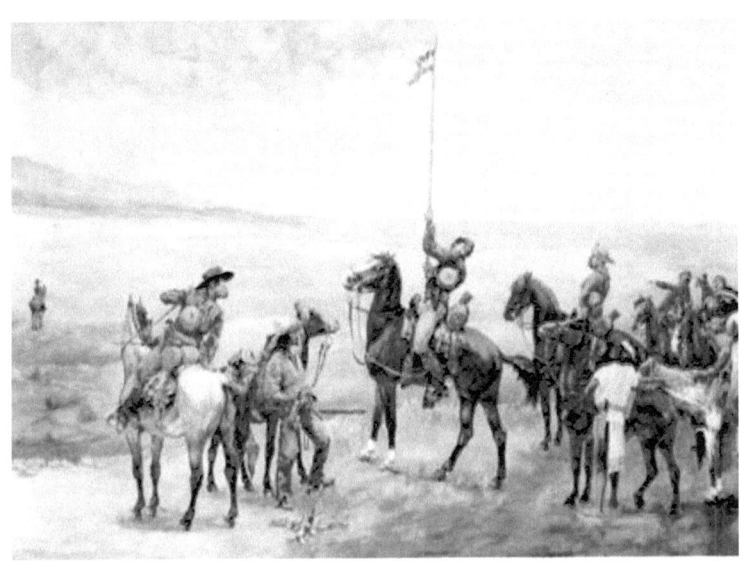

Signaling the Main Command, 1885, watercolor

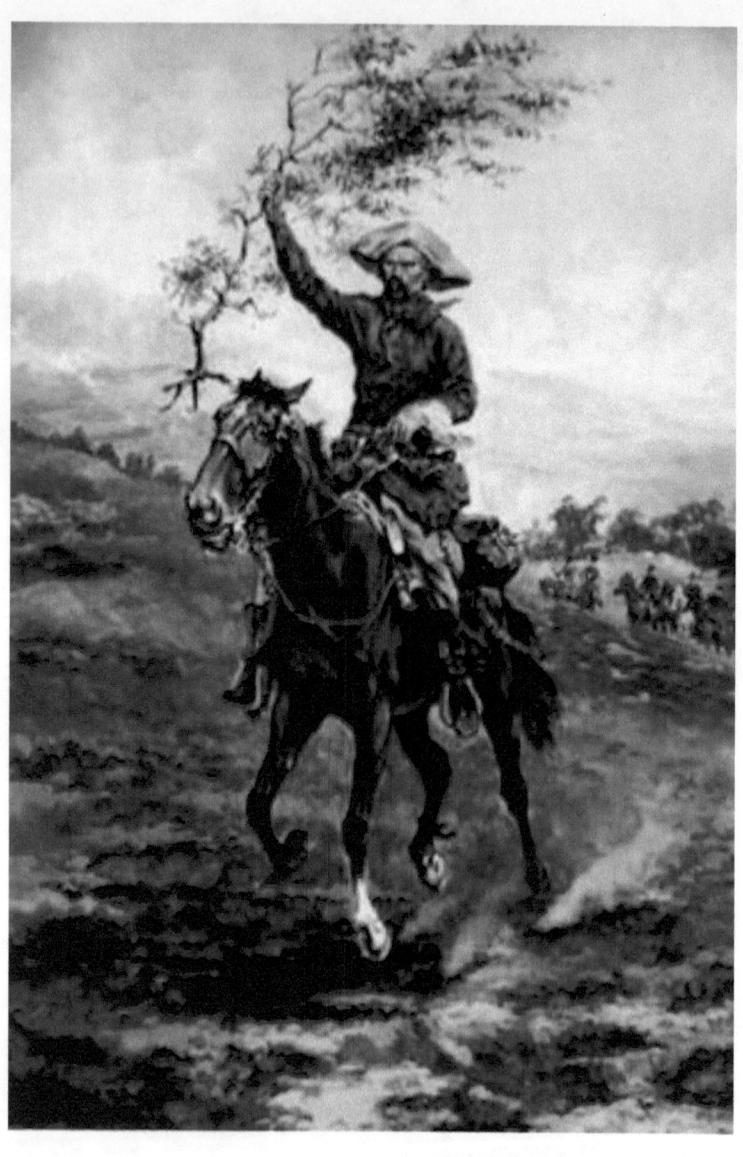

The Flag of Truce in the Indian War, 1886, oil

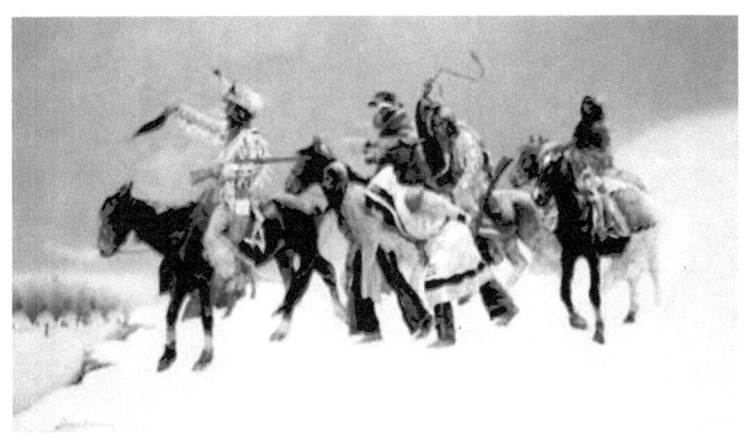

Return of a Blackfoot War Party, 1887, oil

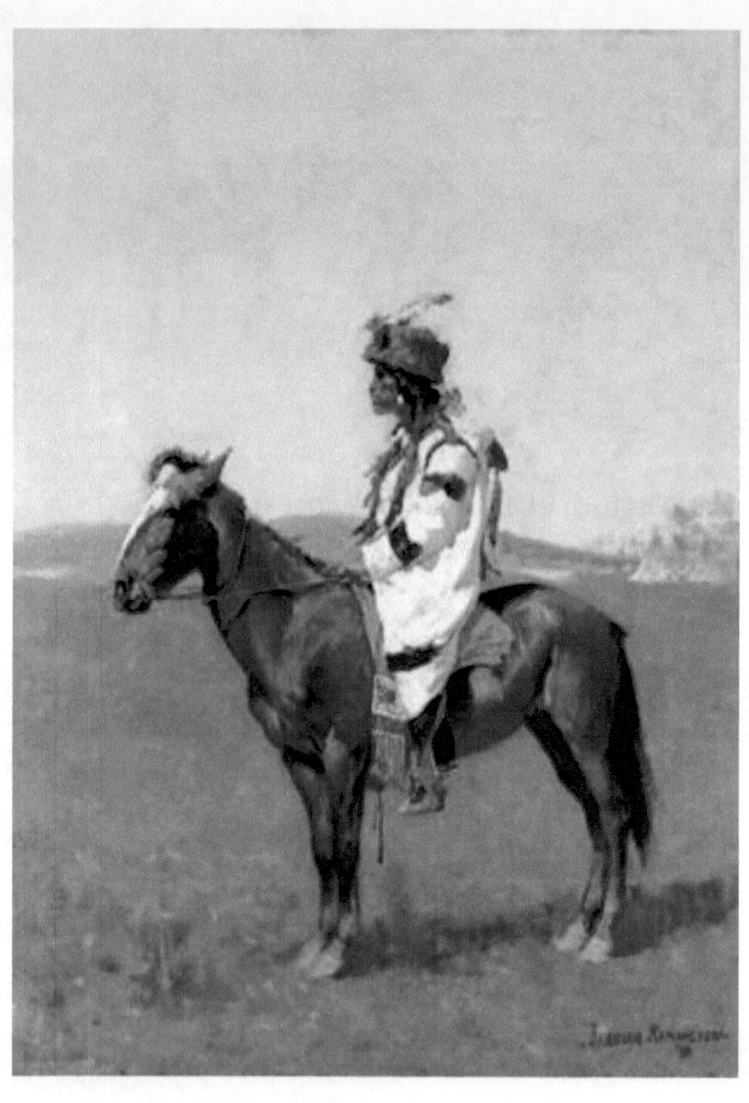

A Blackfoot Chief, 1888, oil

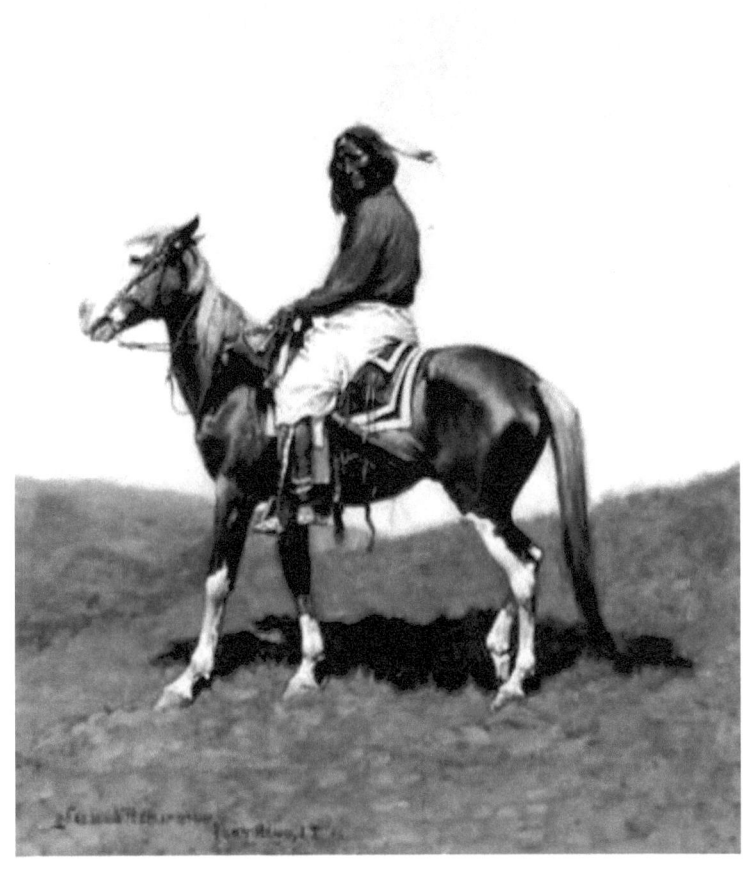

Comanche Brave, Fort Reno, Indian Territory,
1888, oil

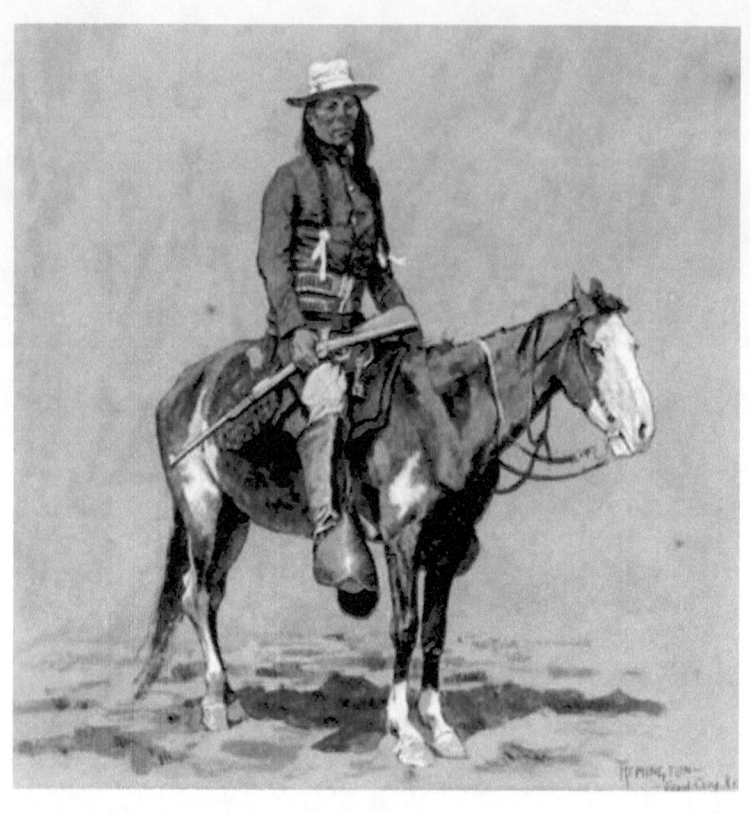

Indian Scout at Fort Reno, 1888, Drawing and gouache on paper

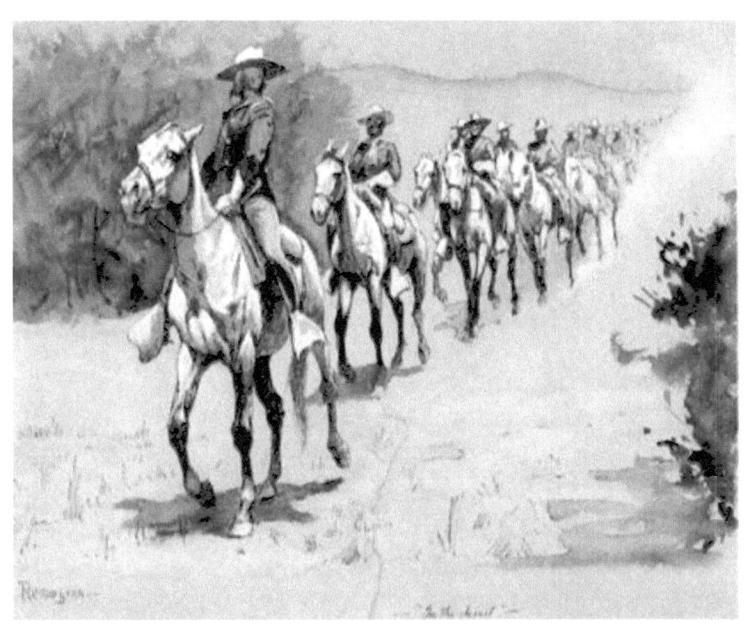

In the Desert, 1888, Pen, Ink wash and gouache
on paper

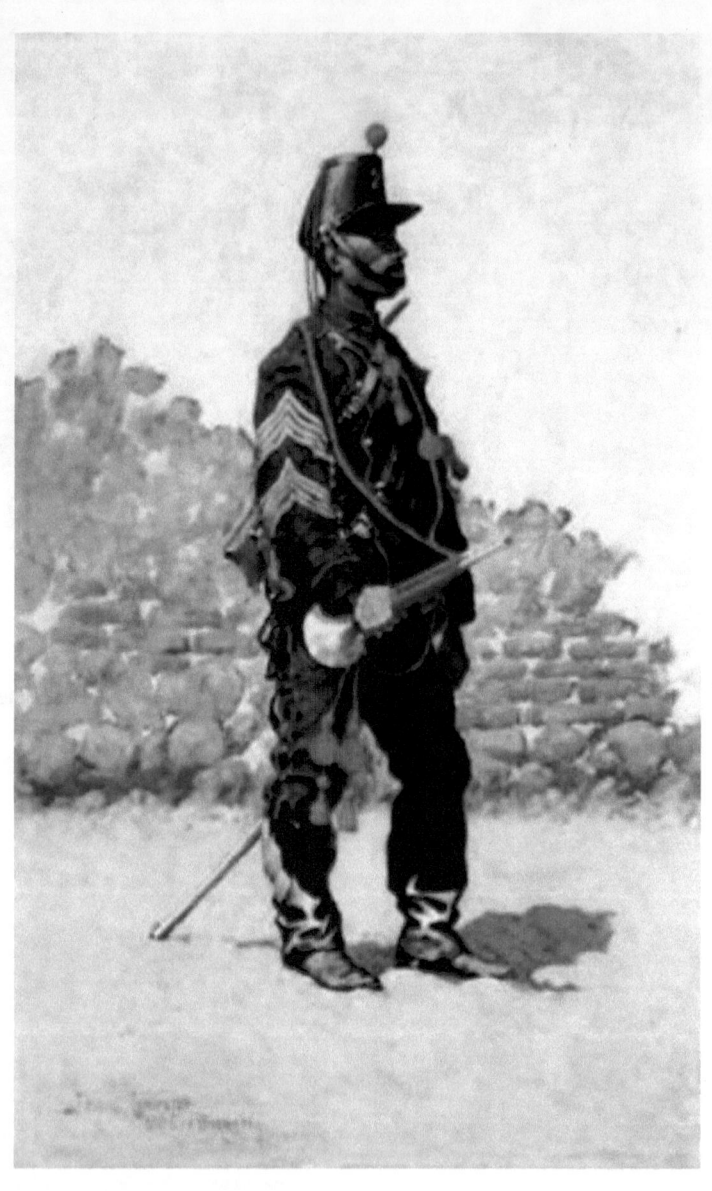

Bugler of Cavalry, 1889, oil

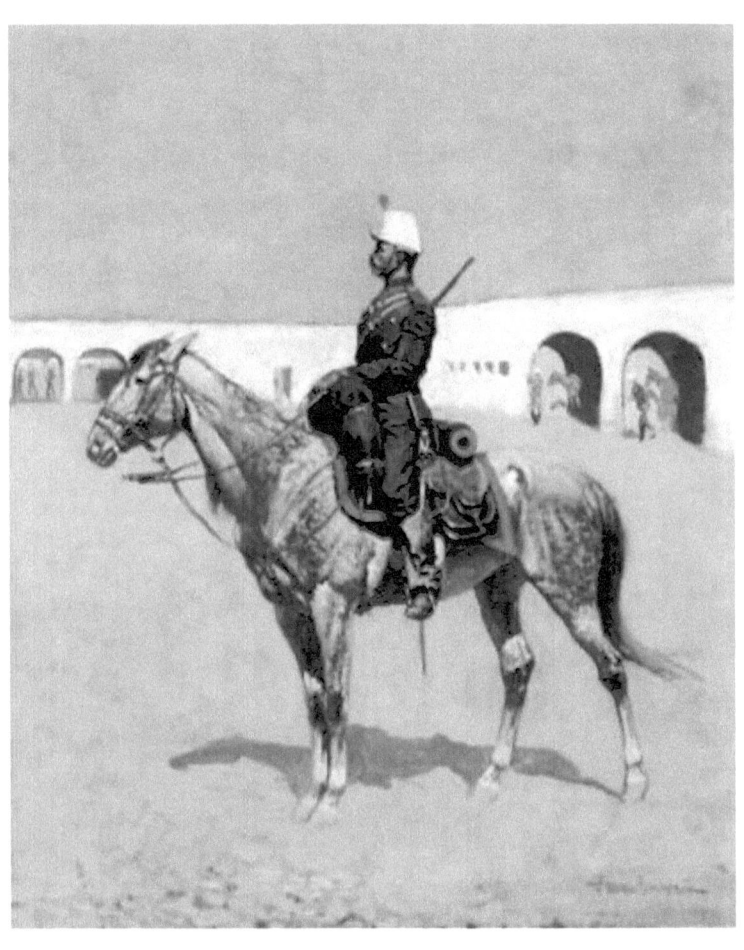

Cavalryman of the Line, Mexico, 1889, oil

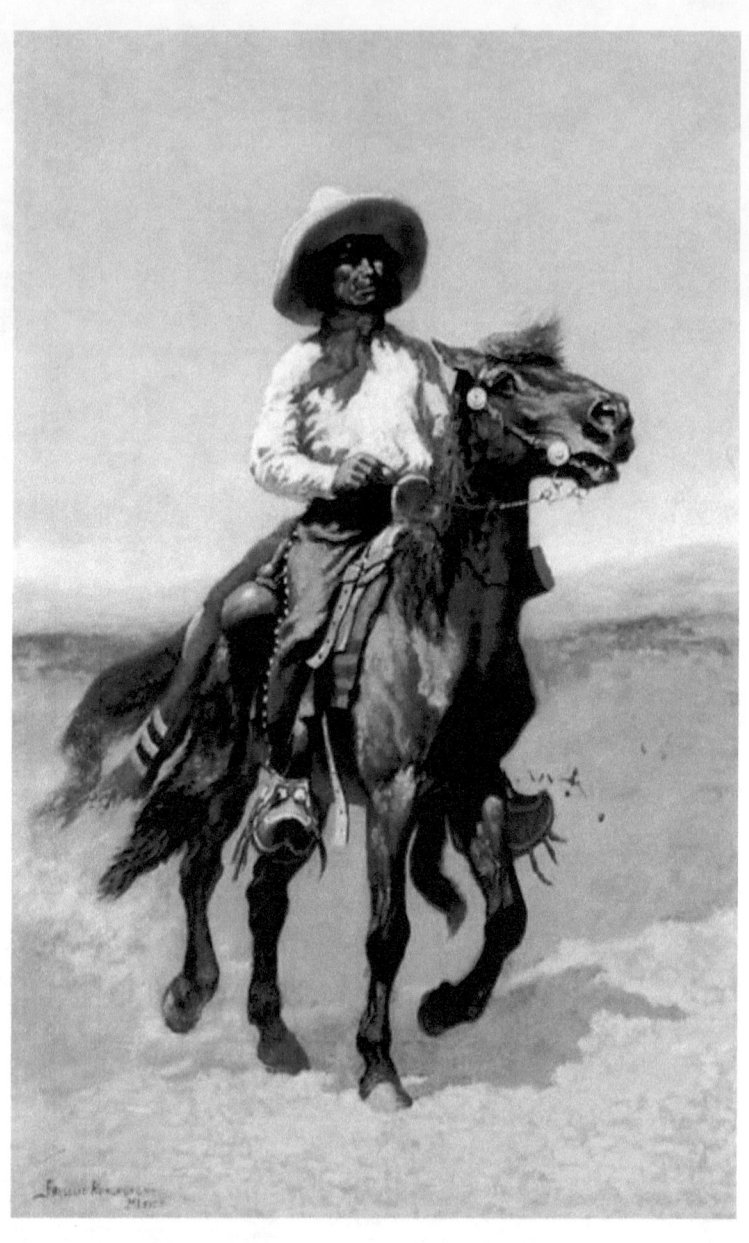

A Regimental Scout, 1889, oil

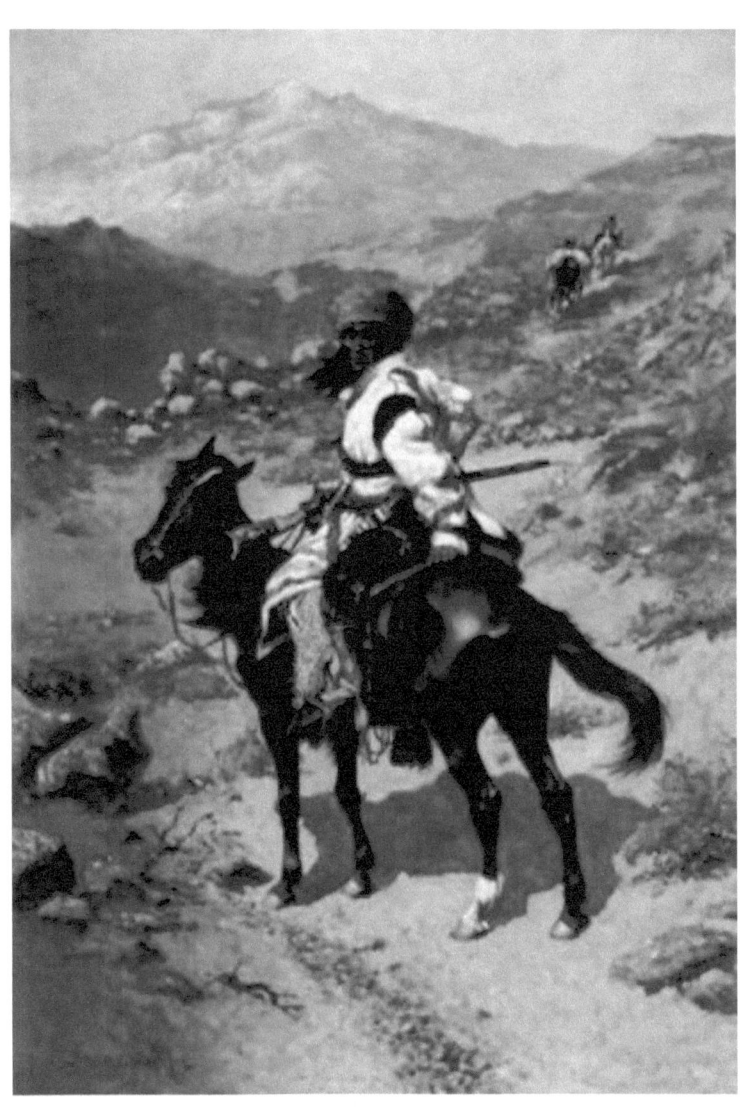

An Indian Trapper, 1889, oil

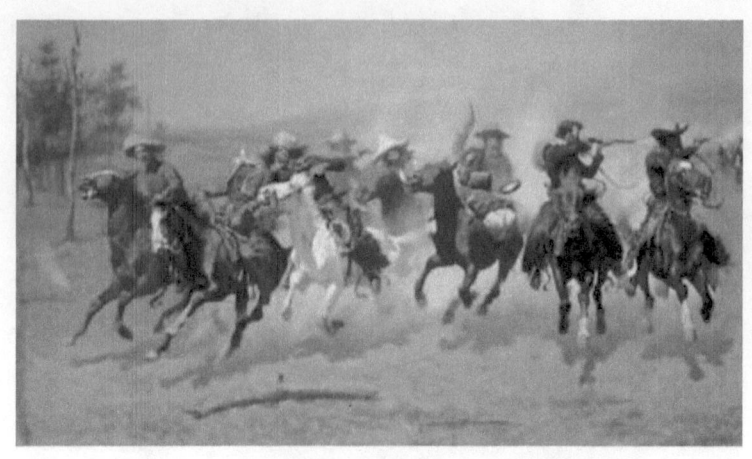

A Dash for the Timber, 1889, oil

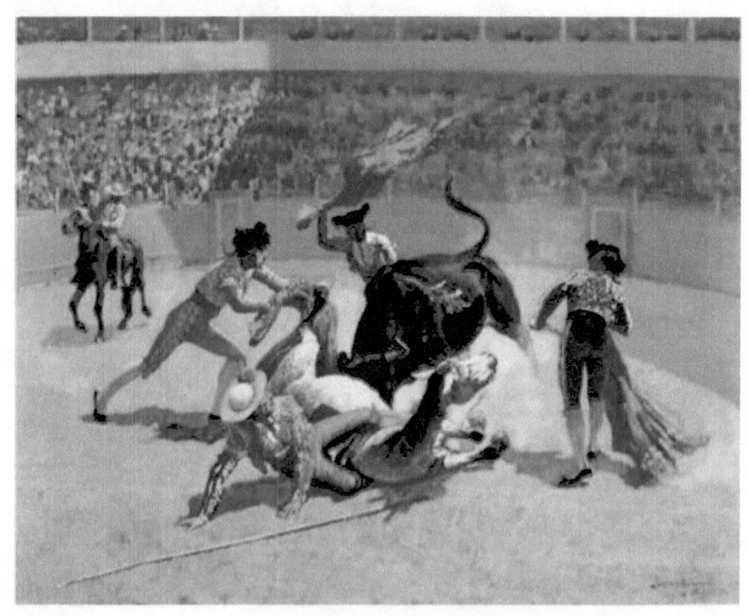

Bull Fight in Mexico, 1889, oil

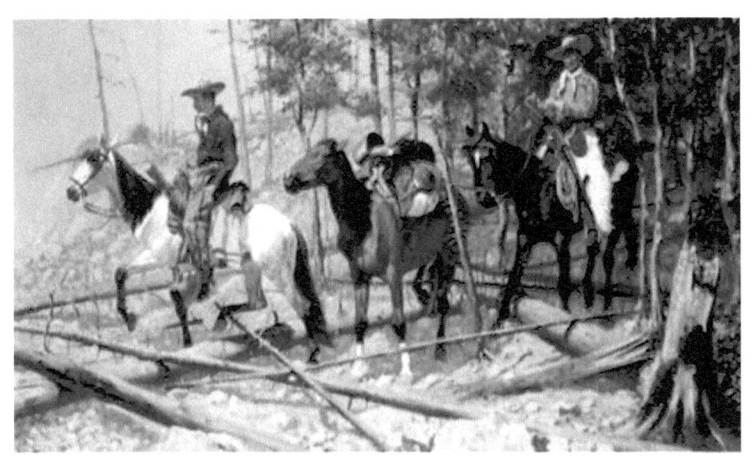

Prospecting for Cattle Range, 1889, oil

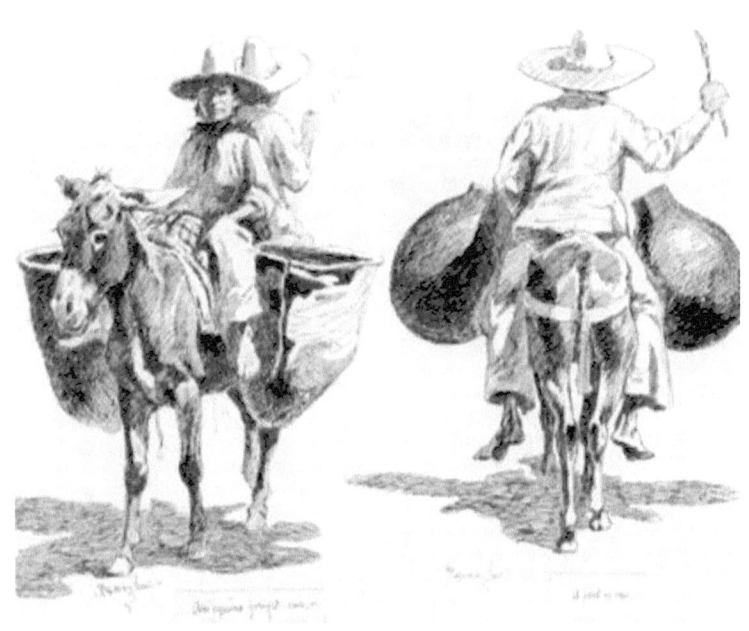

An Equine Freight Car and a Point of View,
1889, pen and ink

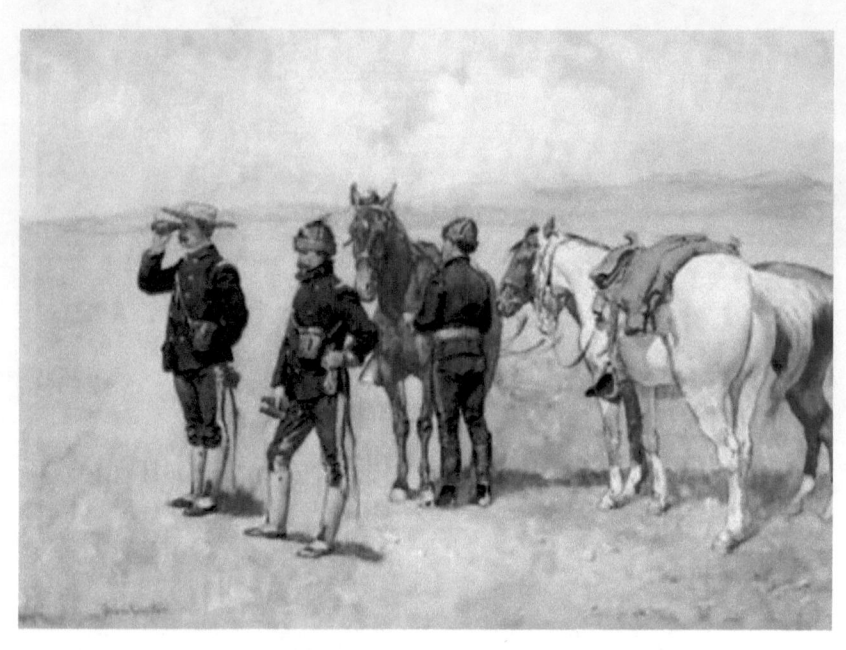

The Scouting Party, 1889, watercolor

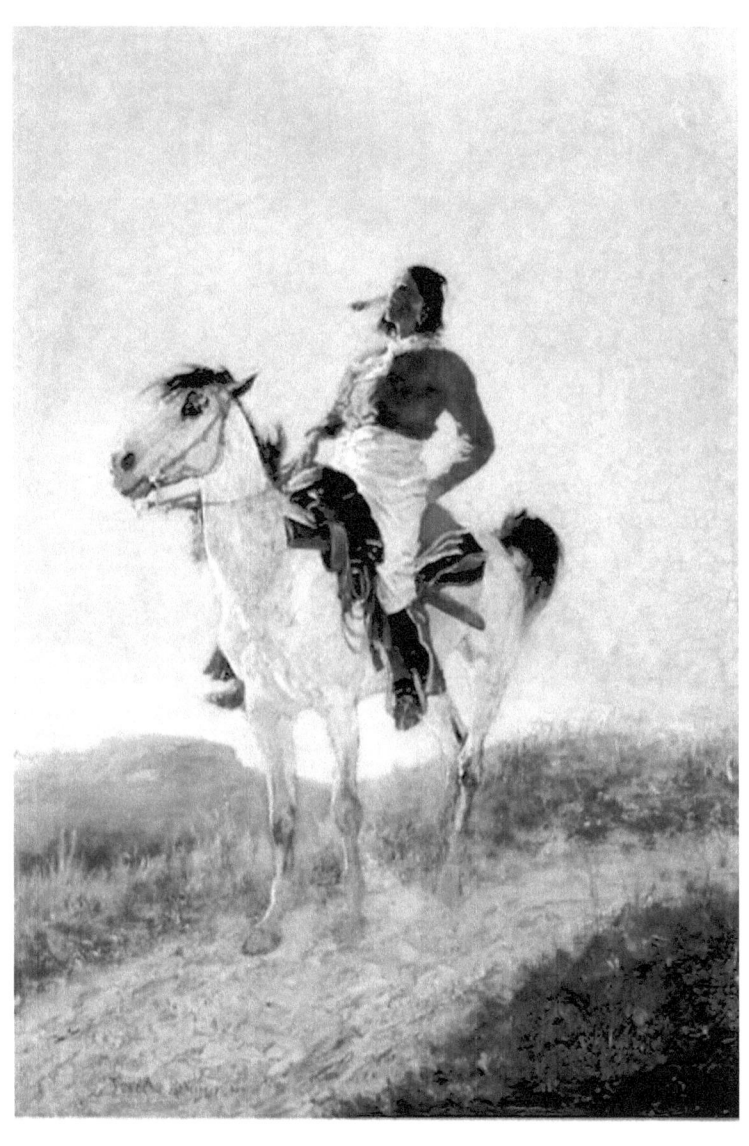

Modern Comanche, 1890, oil

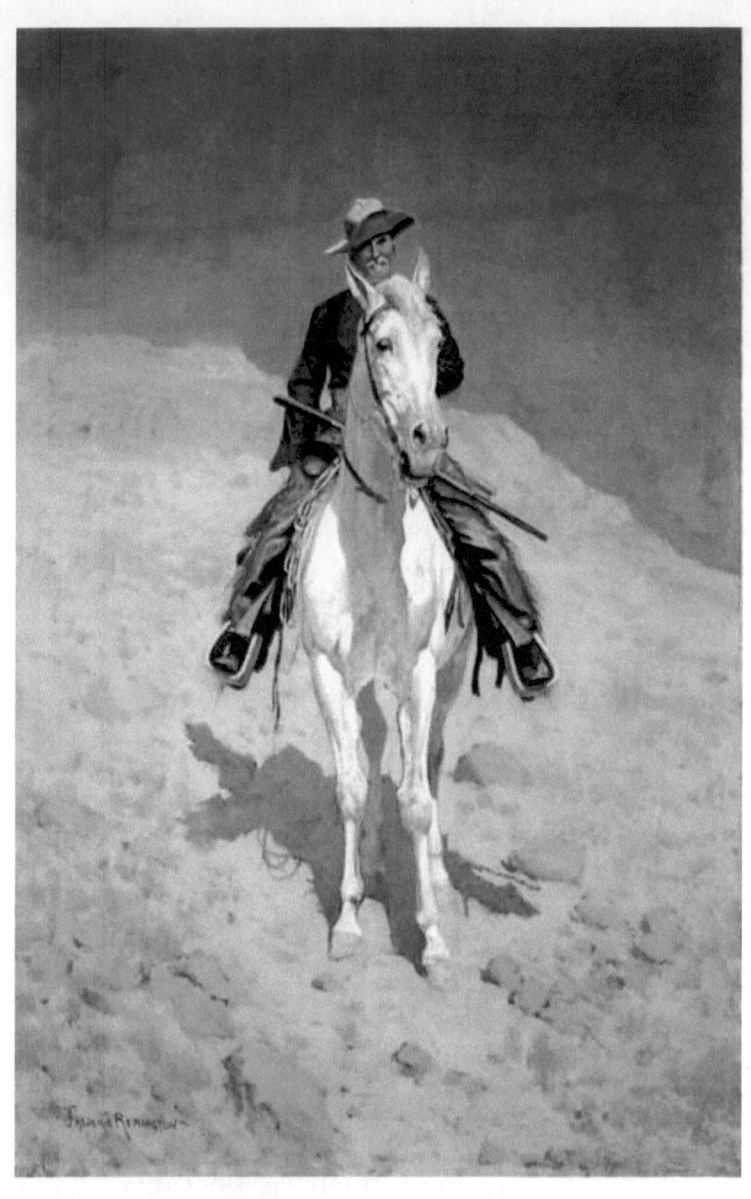

Self-Portrait on a Horse, 1890, oil

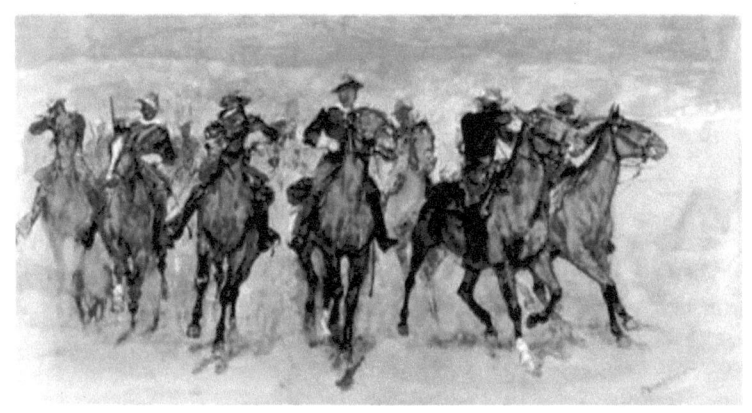

Colored Troopers to the Rescue, 1890, oil

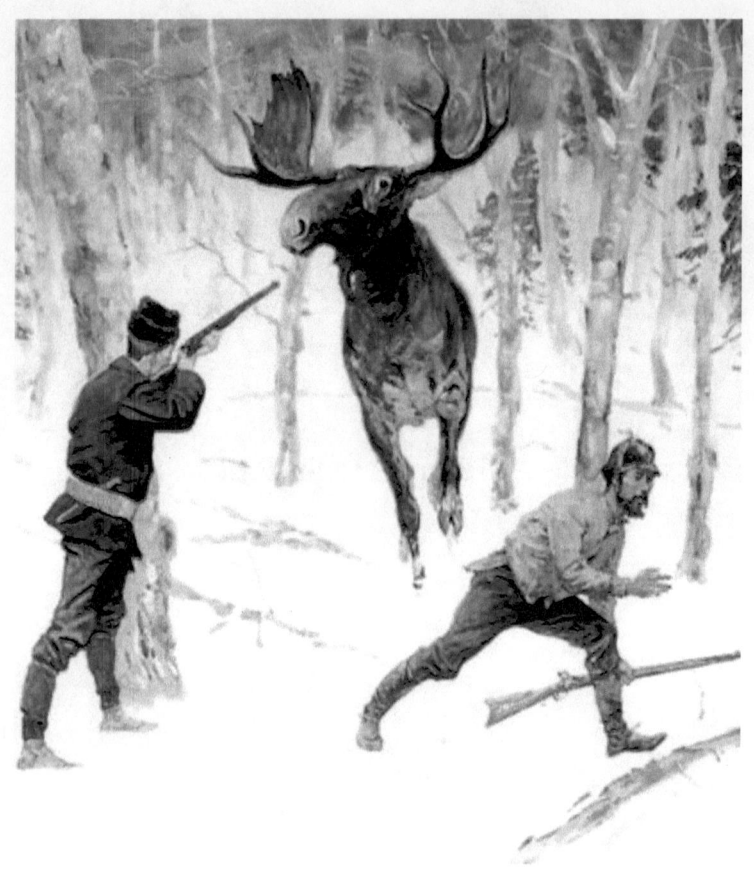

The Moose Hunt, 1890, watercolor

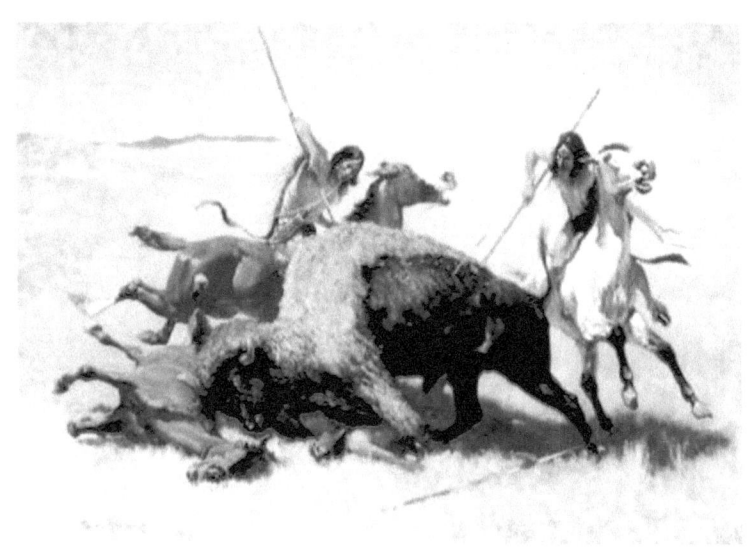

The Buffalo Hunt, 1890, oil

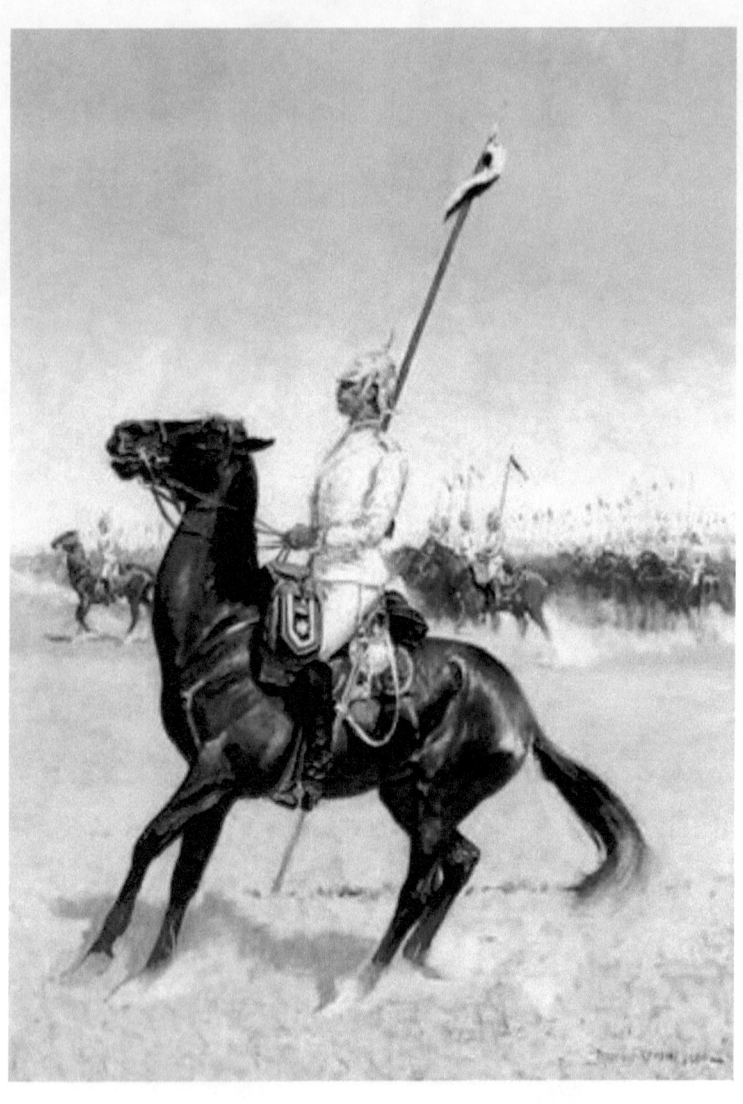

Cuirassiers (also known as Imperial Lancers),
1890, oil

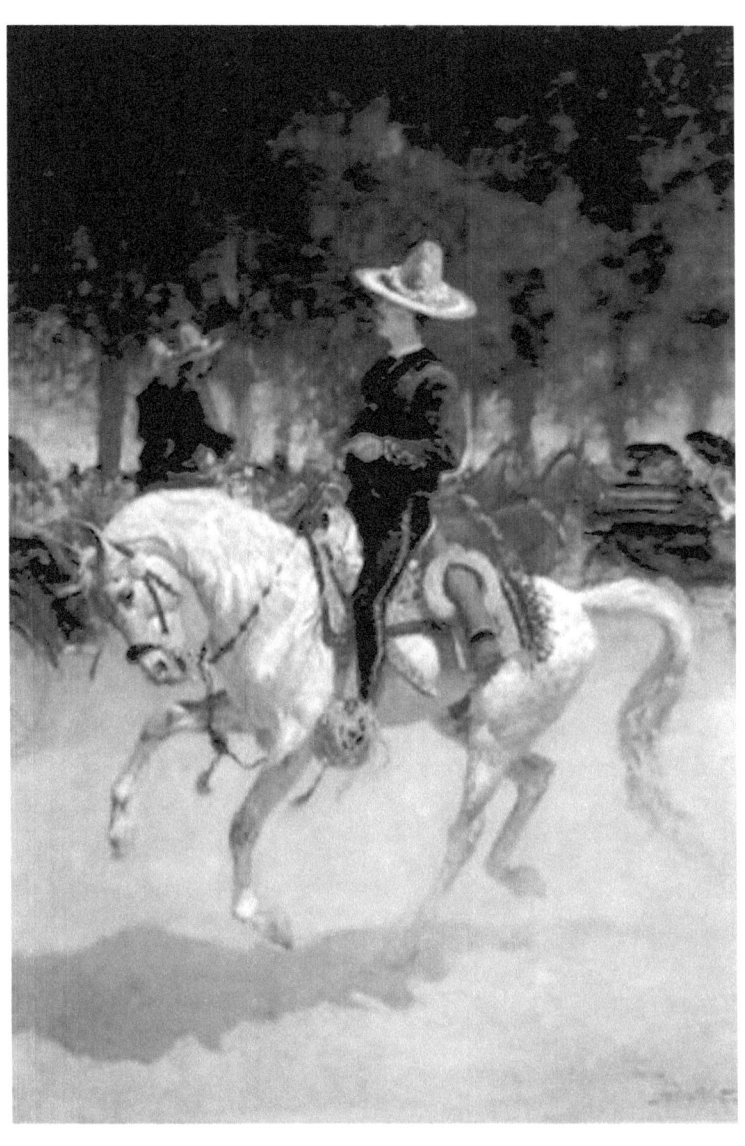

A Dandy on the Paseo de la Reforma, Mexico
City, 1890, oil

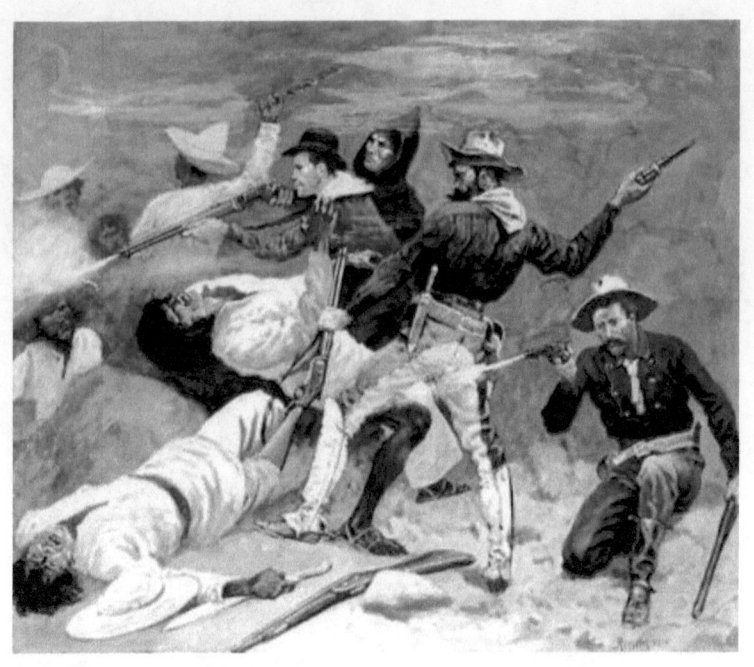

The Fight in the Canyon, 1890, Gouache and ink
on paper

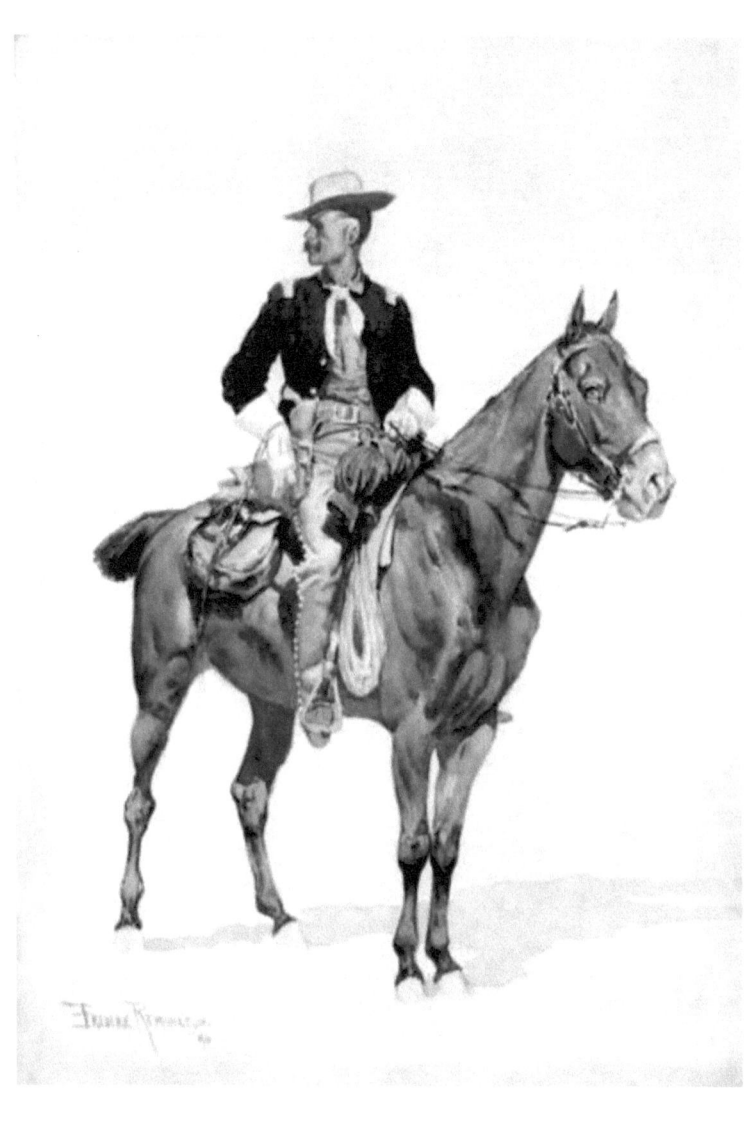

Lieutenant S. C. Robertson, Chief of the Crow
Scouts, 1890, watercolor

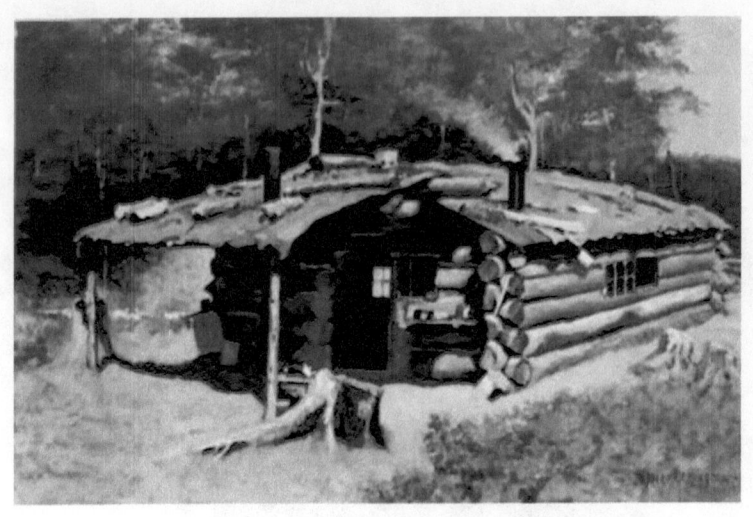

Thompson's Cabin on Silver Lake, 1890, oil

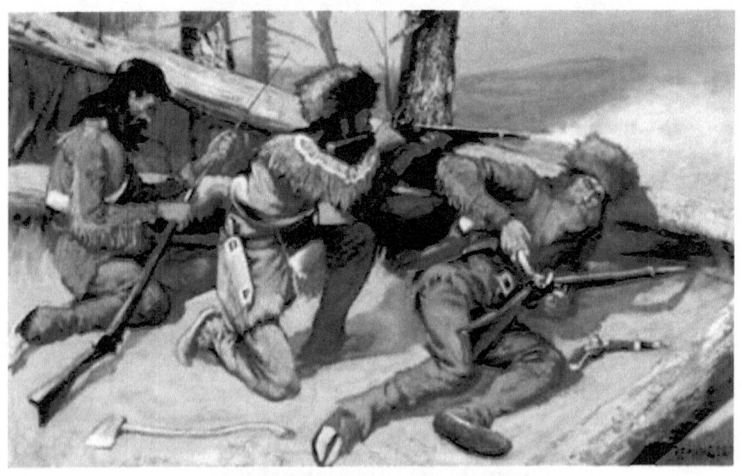

A Brush with the Redskins, 1891, oil

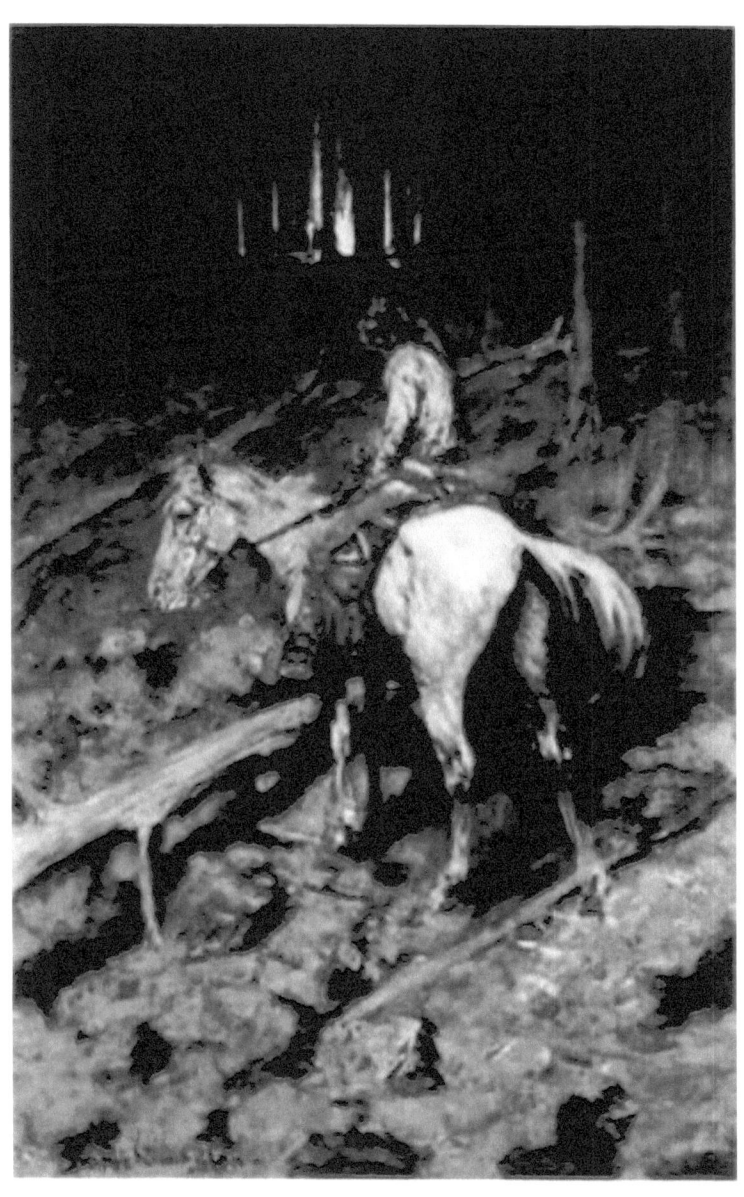

Apache Fire Signal, 1891, oil

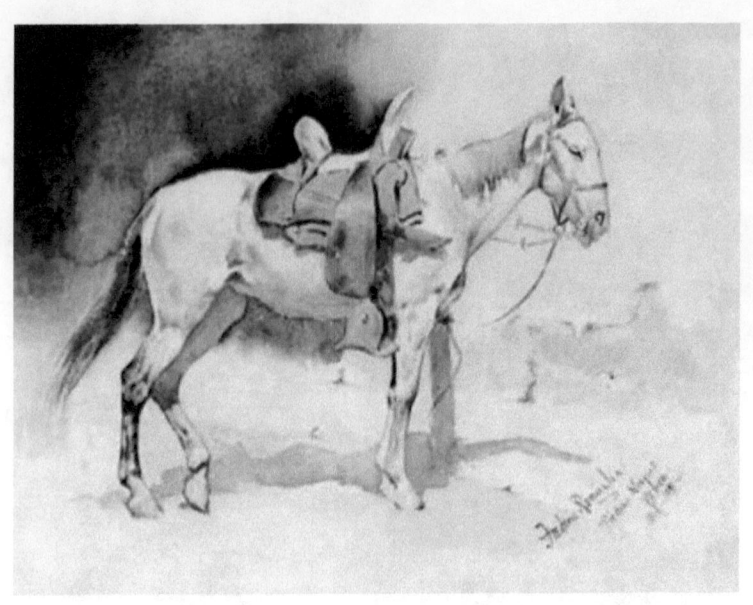

Mexican Pony - Piedras Neagras, 1891,
watercolor

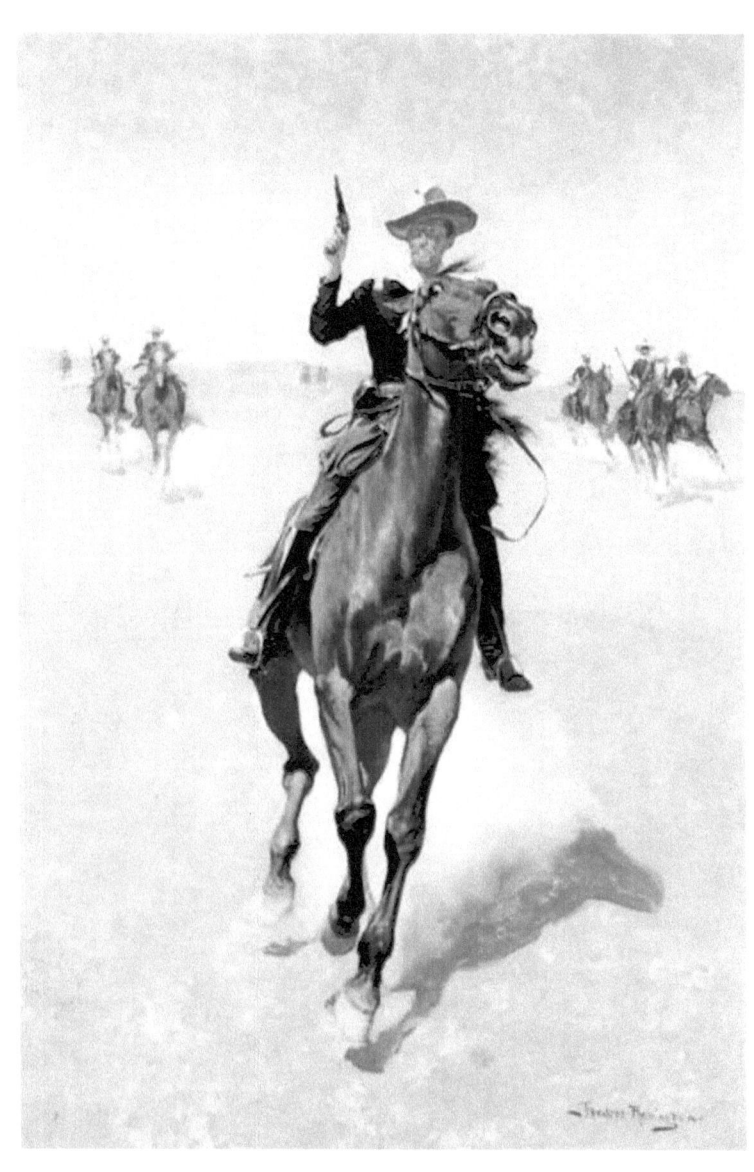

The Trooper, 1892, oil

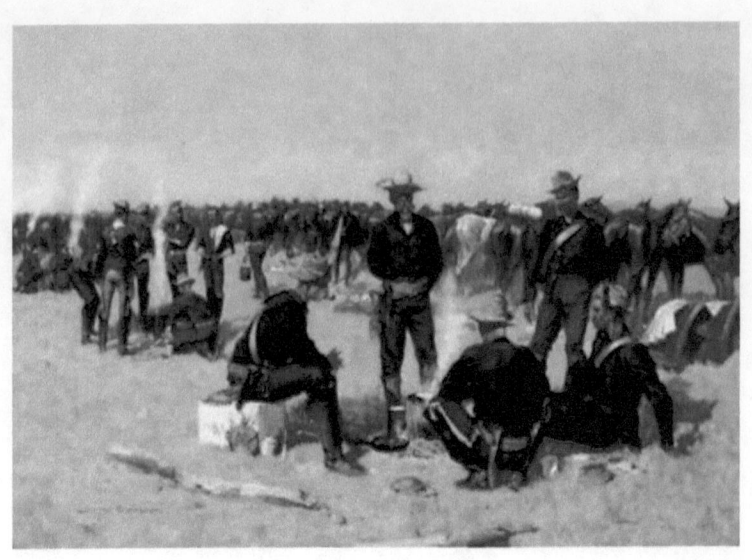

A Cavalryman's Breakfast on the Plains, 1892, oil

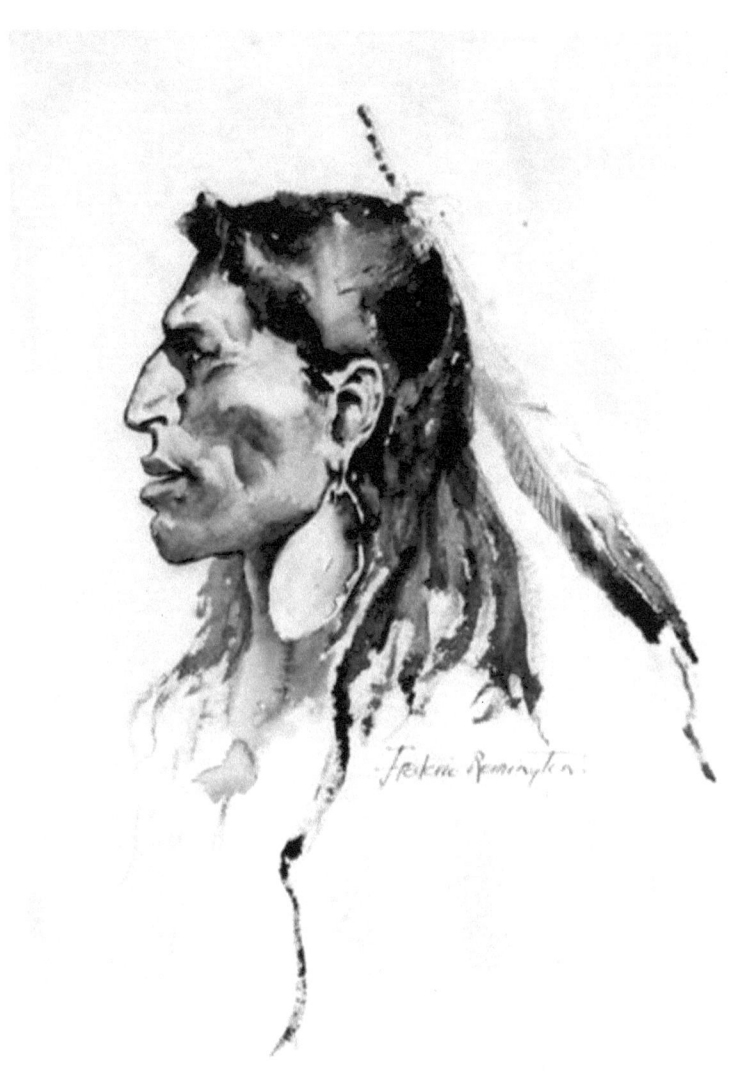

The Cheyenne Type, 1892, Ink and in was on
prepared paper

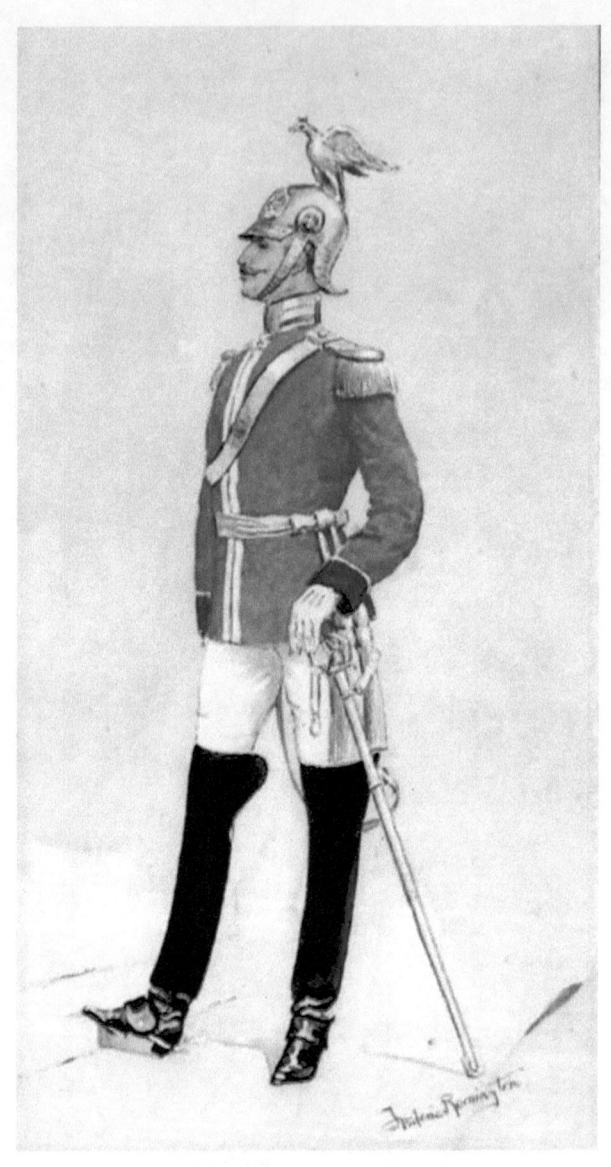

Cuirassier, 1892, watercolor

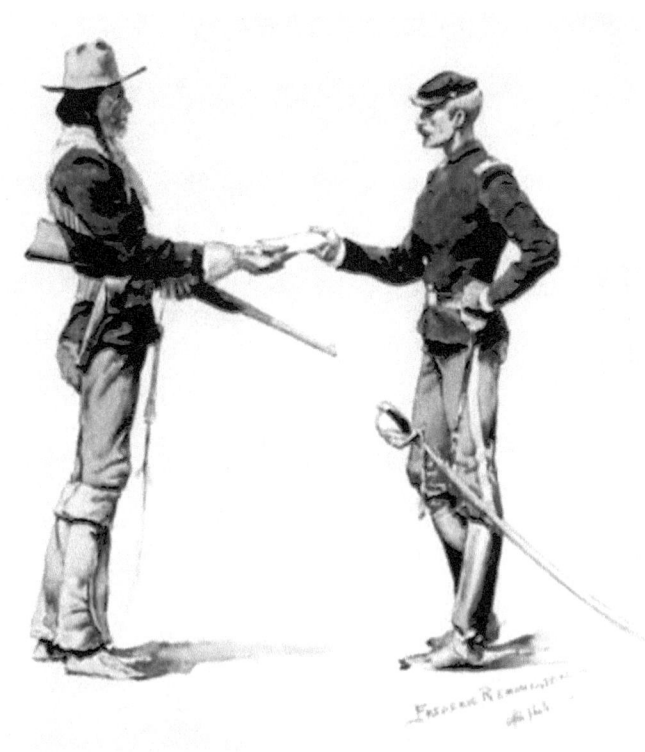

The Dispatch Bearer Troop B, United States
Scouts, 1892, Ink and ink wash on prepared board

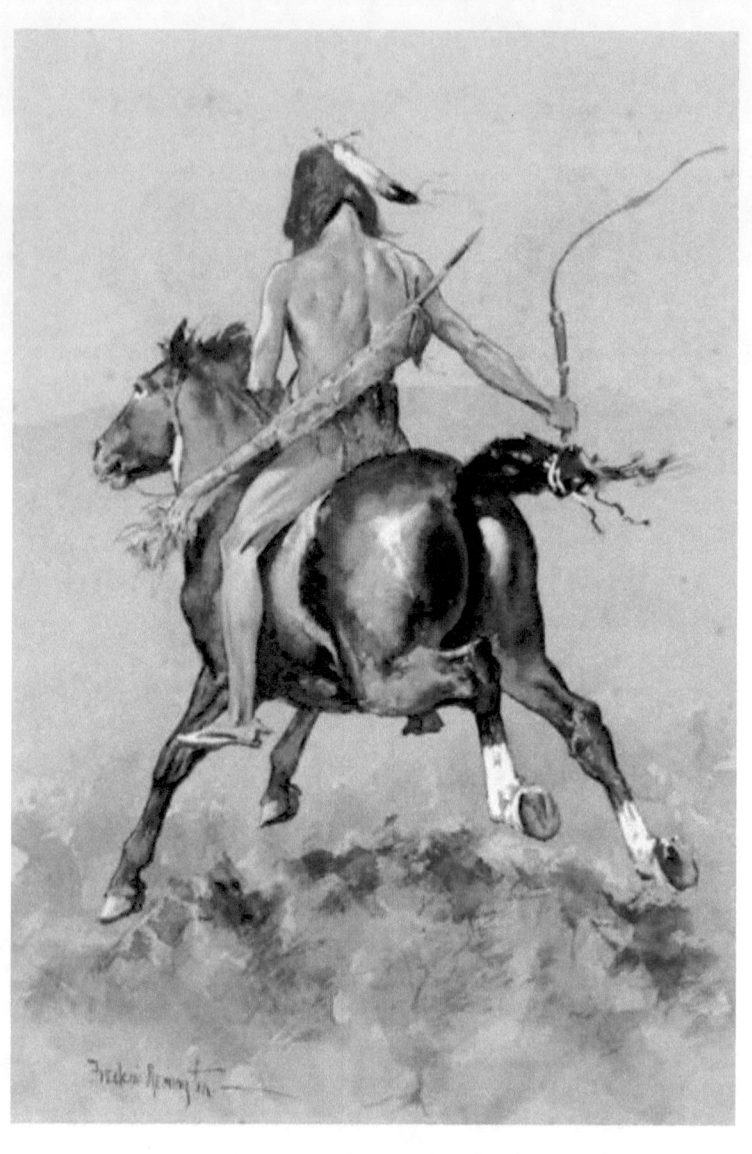

Going to the Buffalo Hunt, 1892, Ink and wash
on paper

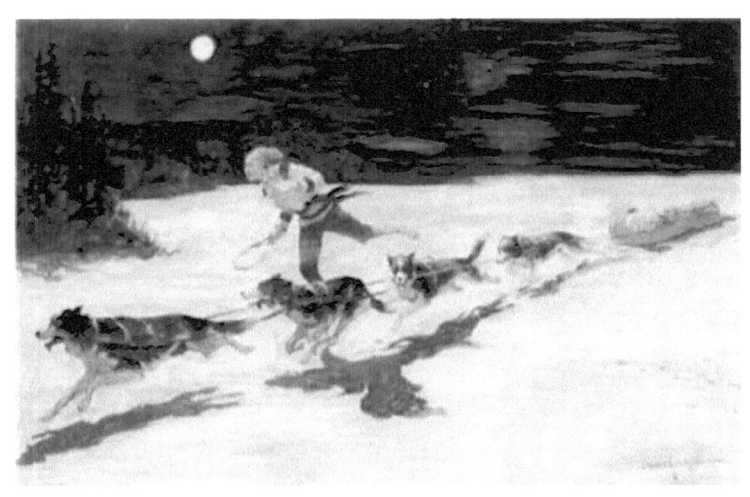

Huskie Dogs on the Frozen highway, 1892,
watercolor and gouache on paper

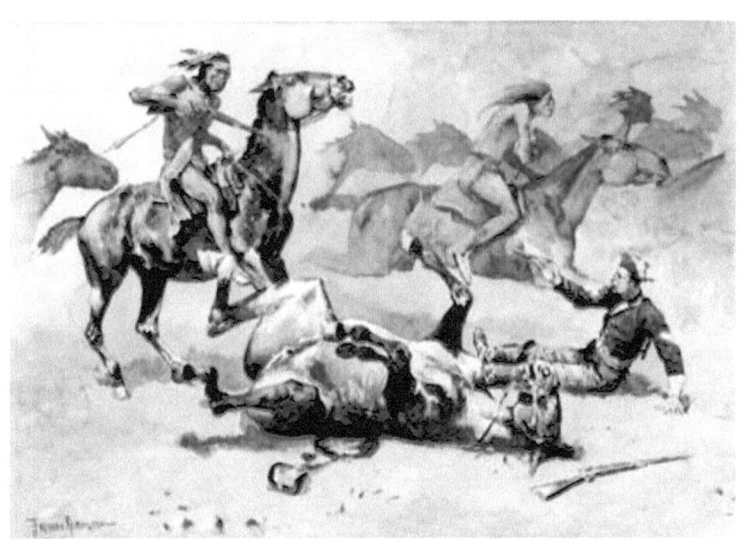

Unhorsed, 1892, India ink and ink was on paper

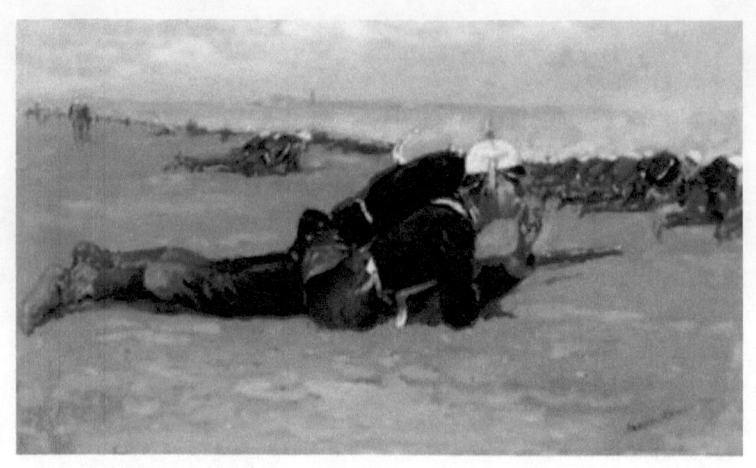

Field Drill for the Prussian Infantry, 1893, oil

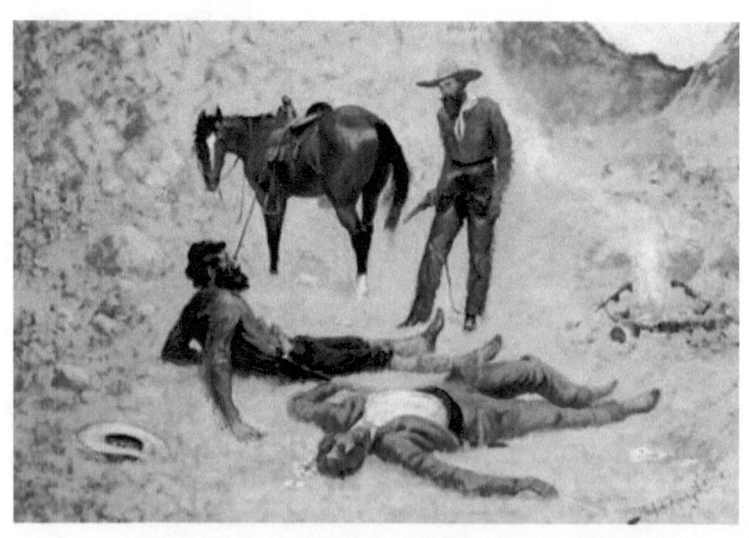

He Lay Where He Had Been Jerked, Still as a
Log, 1893, oil

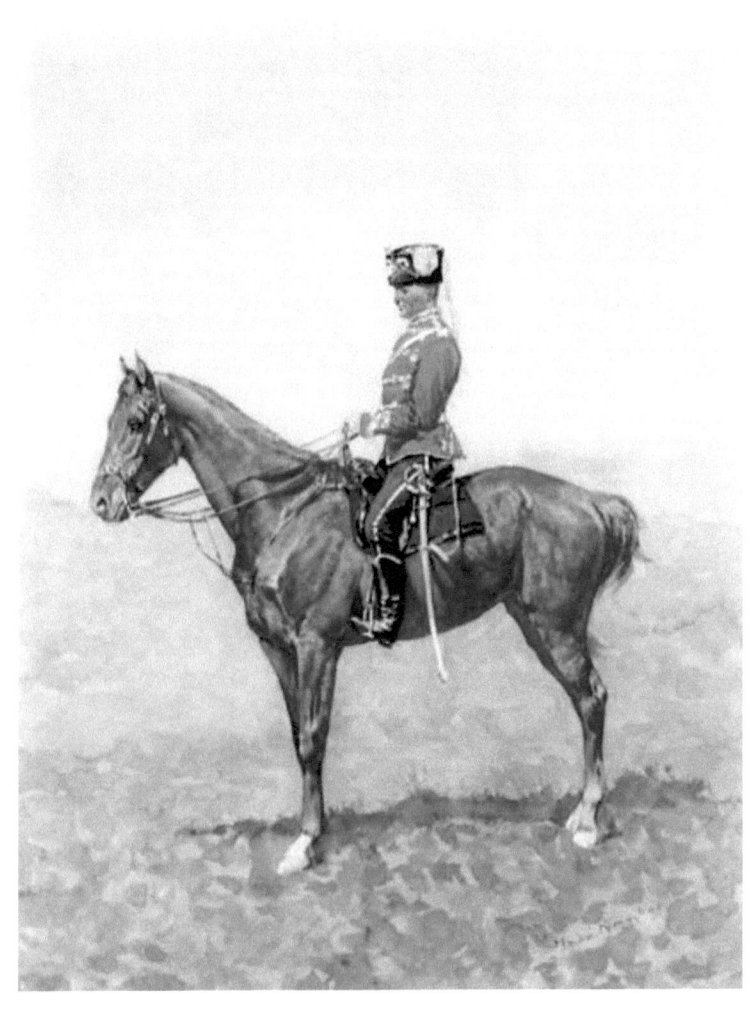

Prussian Calvary Officer on Horseback, 1893, watercolor

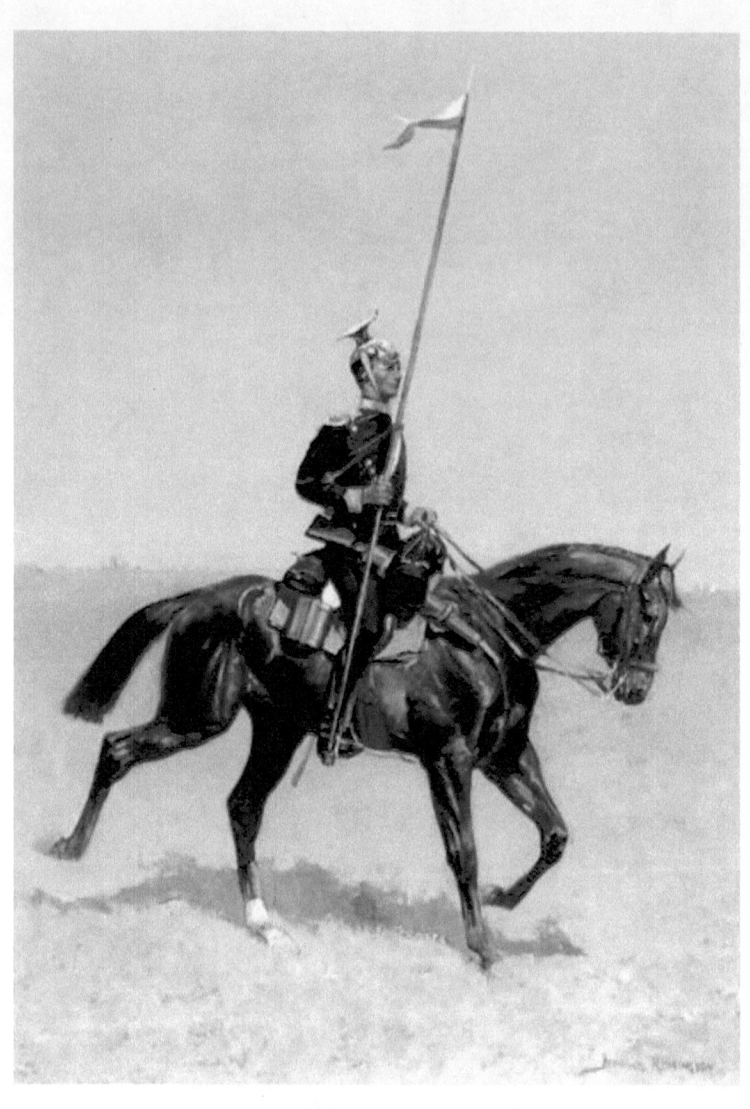

Uhlan (also known as Lancer), 1893, oil

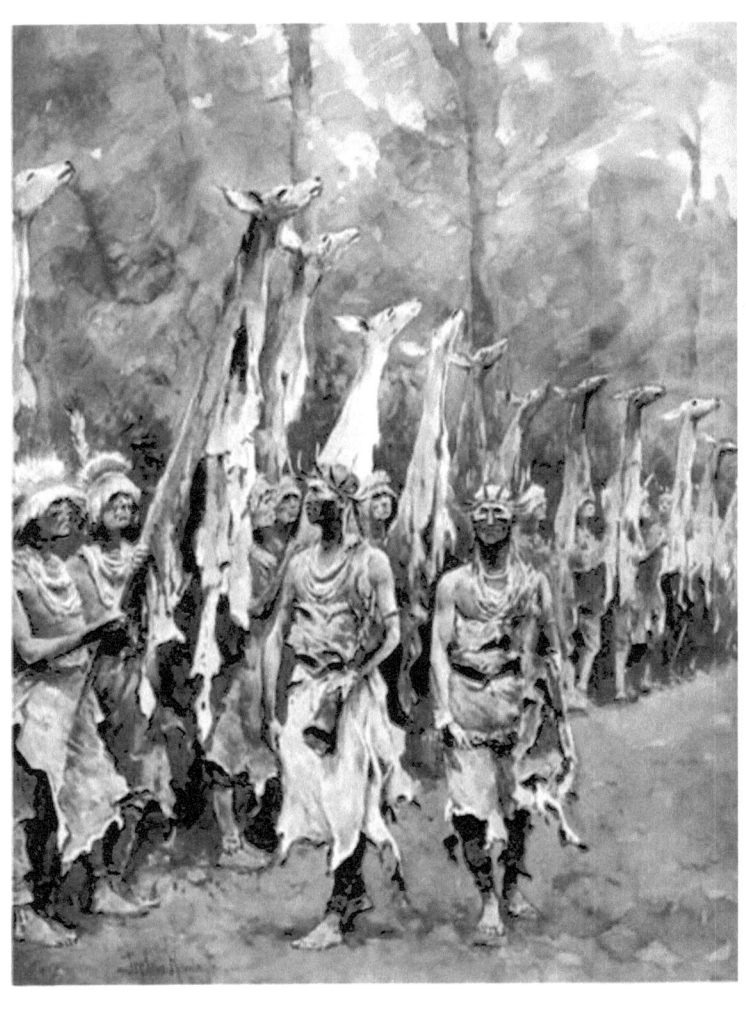

White Deerskin Dance, 1893, Ink and wash on paper

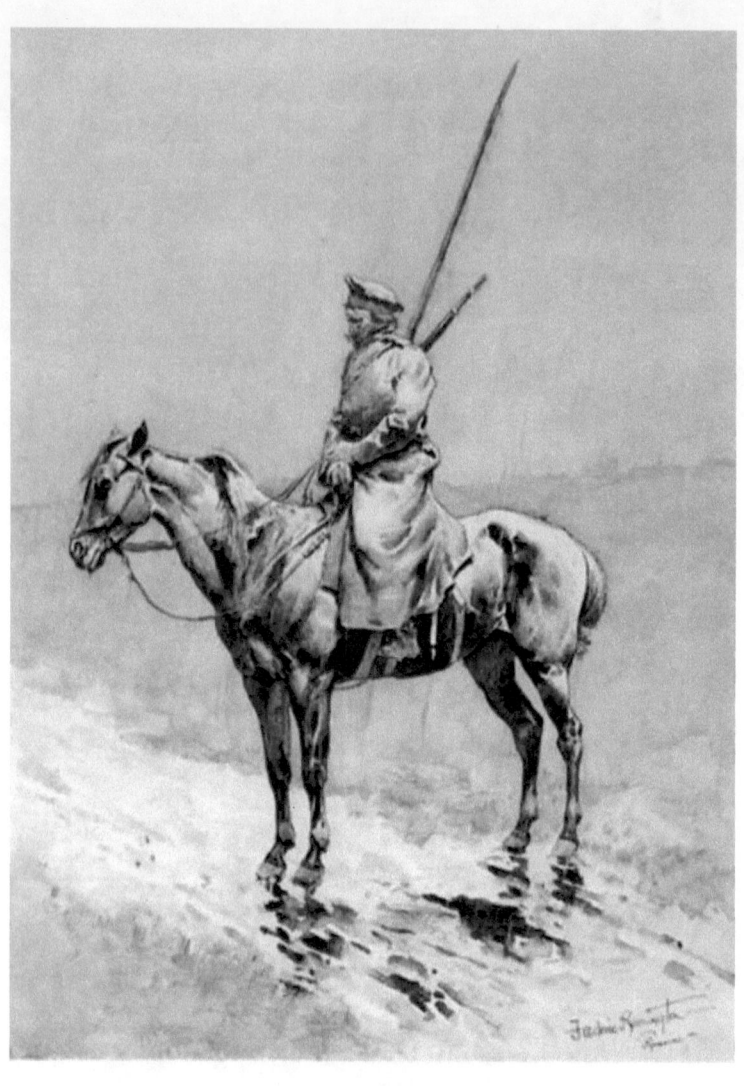

Cossack Picket on the German Frontier, 1894,
watercolor

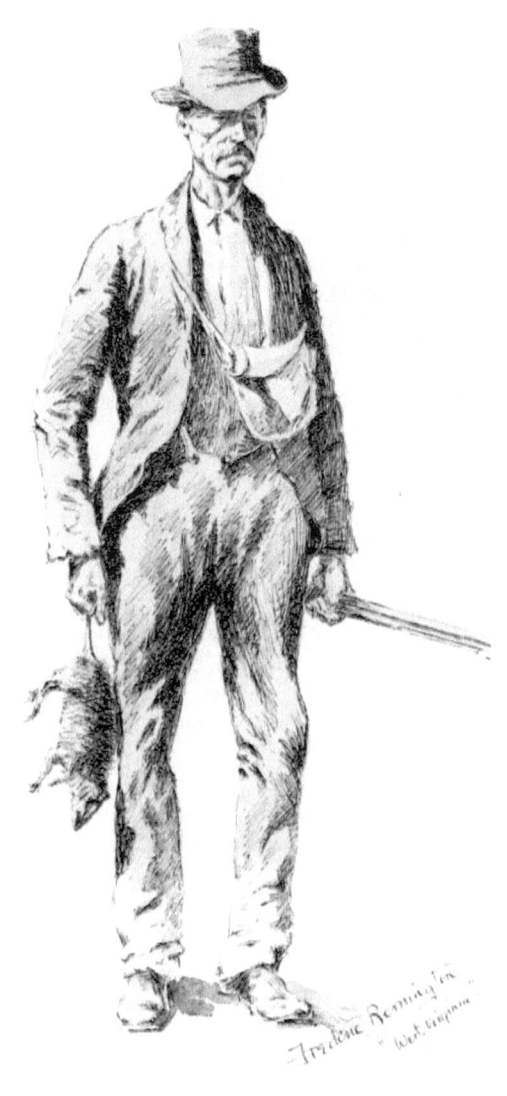

A Native Sportsman (also known as The
'Possom Hunter'), 1894, watercolor and ink on paper

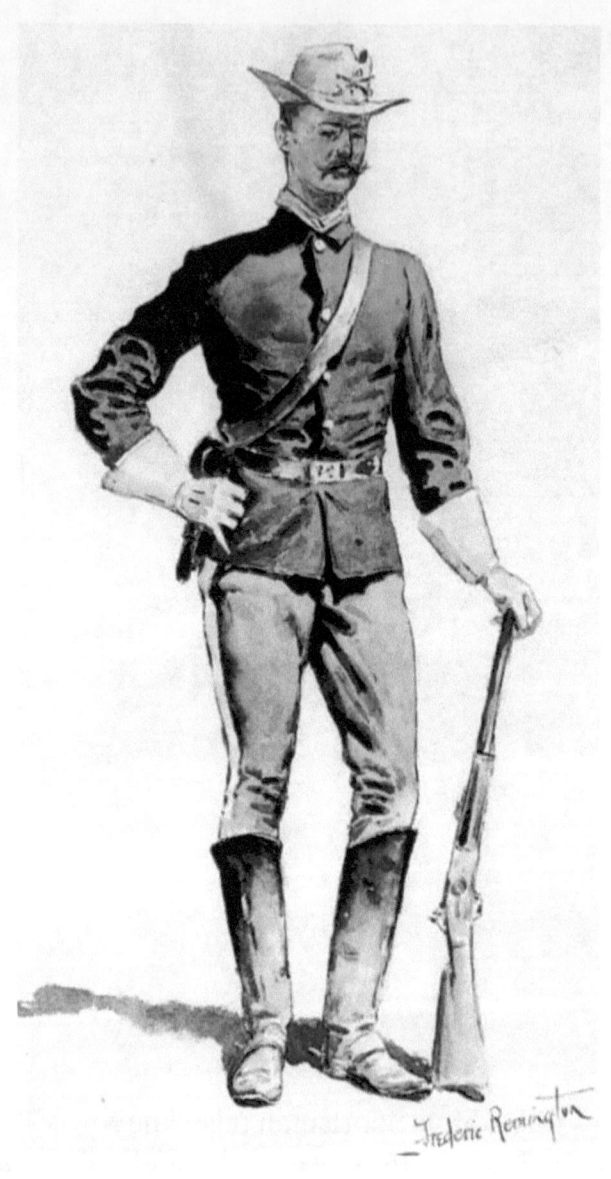

A Trooper, 1894, watercolor and gouache on paper

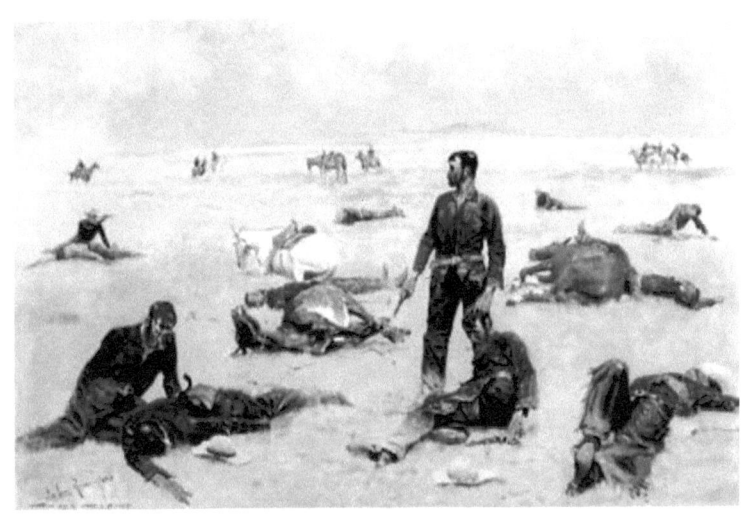

What an Unbranded Cow Has Cost, 1895, oil

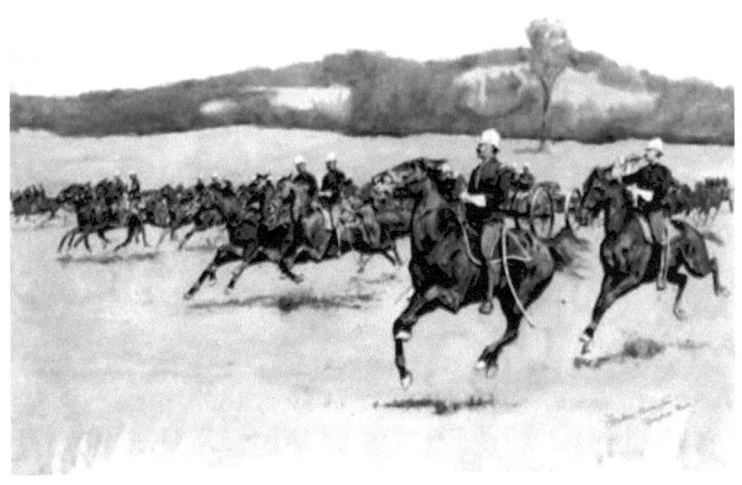

Battery K at Drill in the Berkshire Hills,
Massachusetts, 1895, pen, ink and gouache on paper

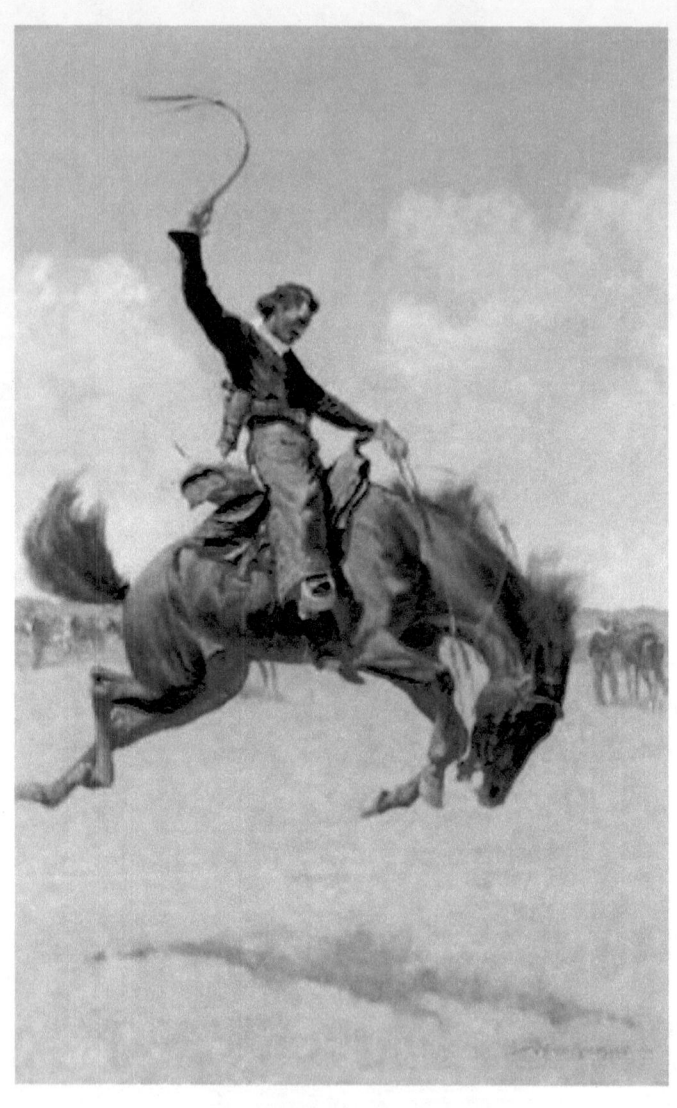

The Bronco Buster, 1895, oil

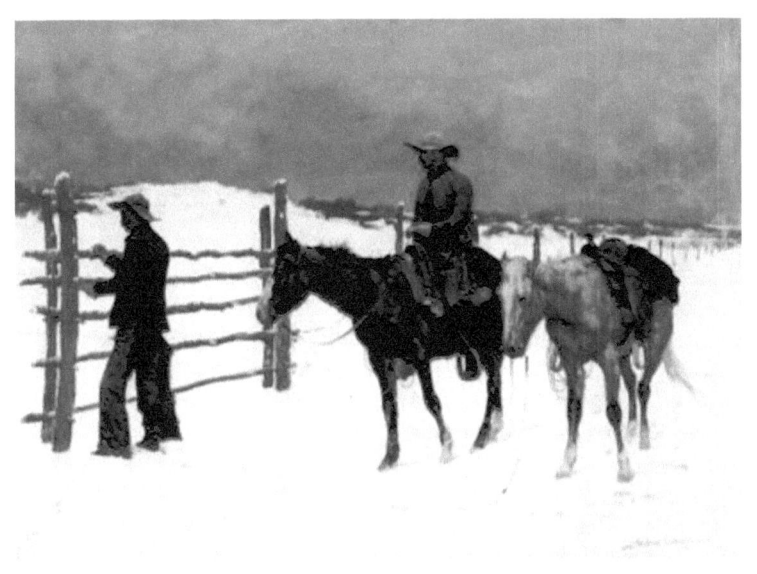

The fall of the Cowboy, 1895, oil

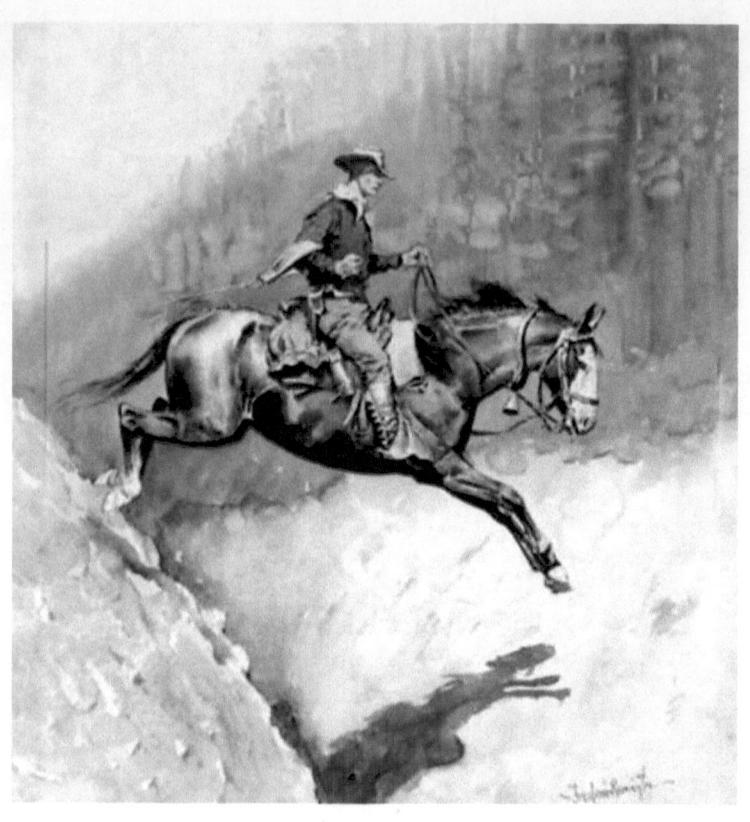

The Bell-Mare over a bad place, 1895, Ink and
ink wash on paper

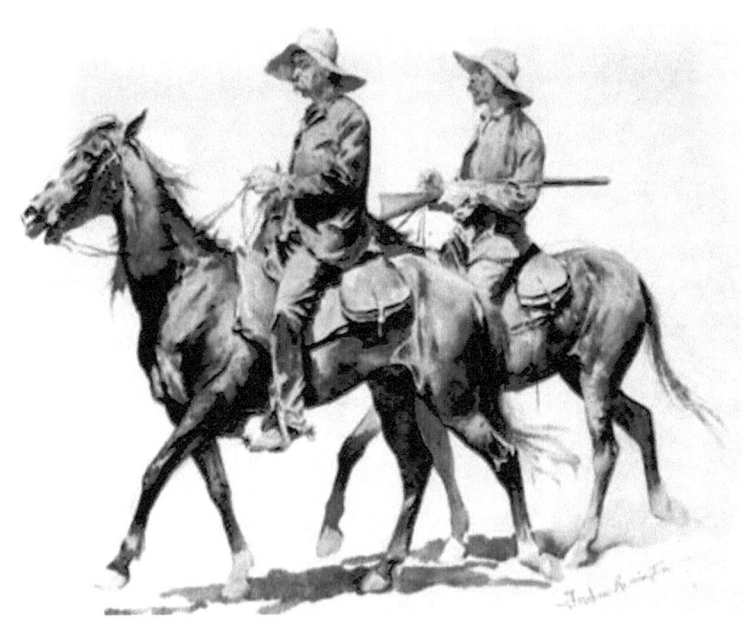

Cracker Cowboys of Florida, 1895, watercolor

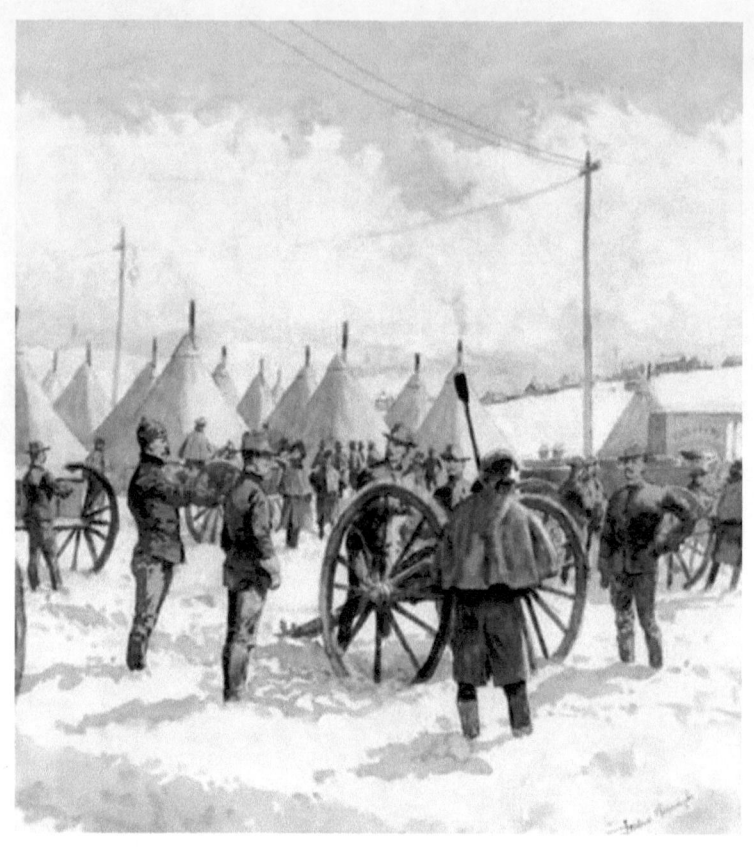

Leadville's Determined Strike - The Denver City
Battery at Camp McIntire, 1896, watercolor

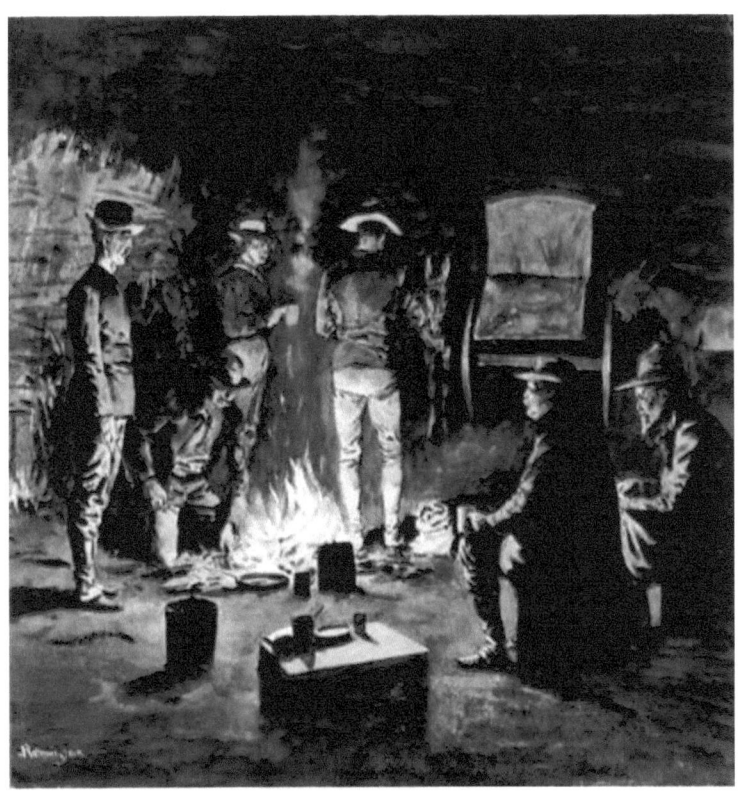

Supper in the Corral (also known as Camp-fire
Texas), 1896, Ink wash with white on paper

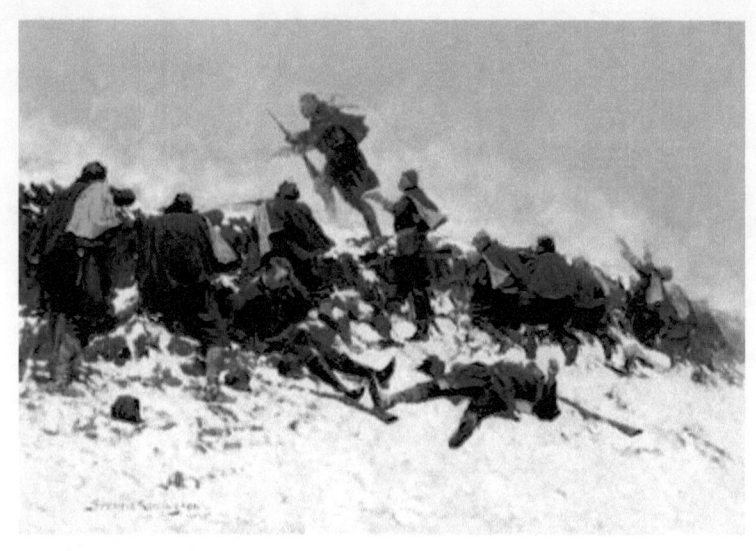

Through the Smoke Sprang the Daring Soldier,
1897, oil

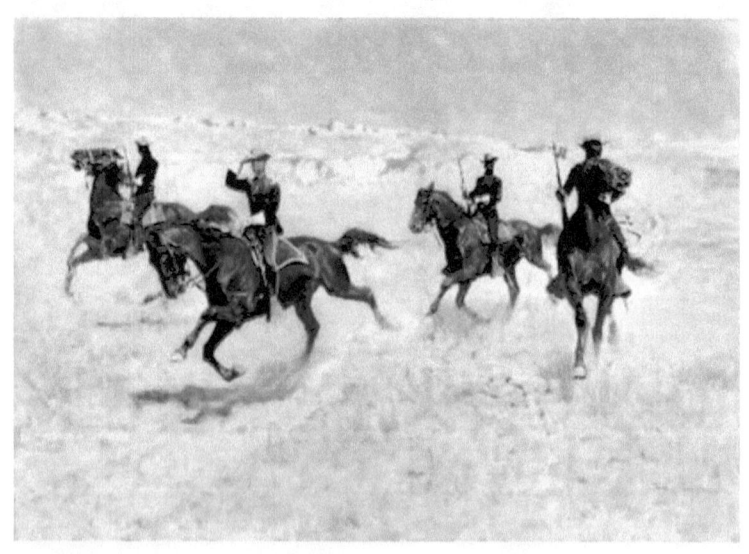

The Advance, 1898, oil

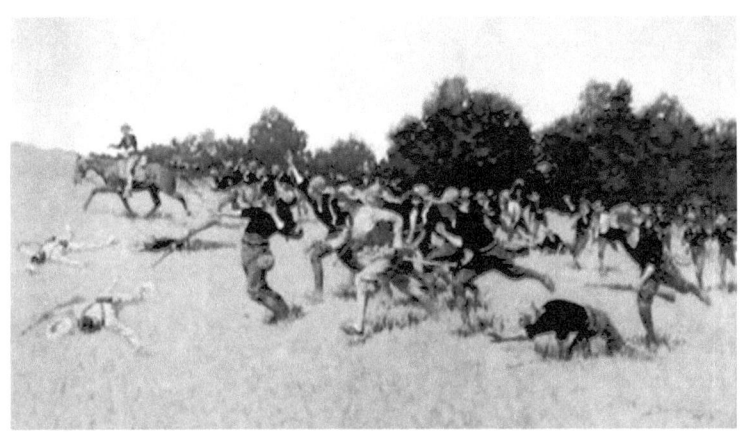

Charge of the Rough Riders at San Juan Hill,
1898, oil

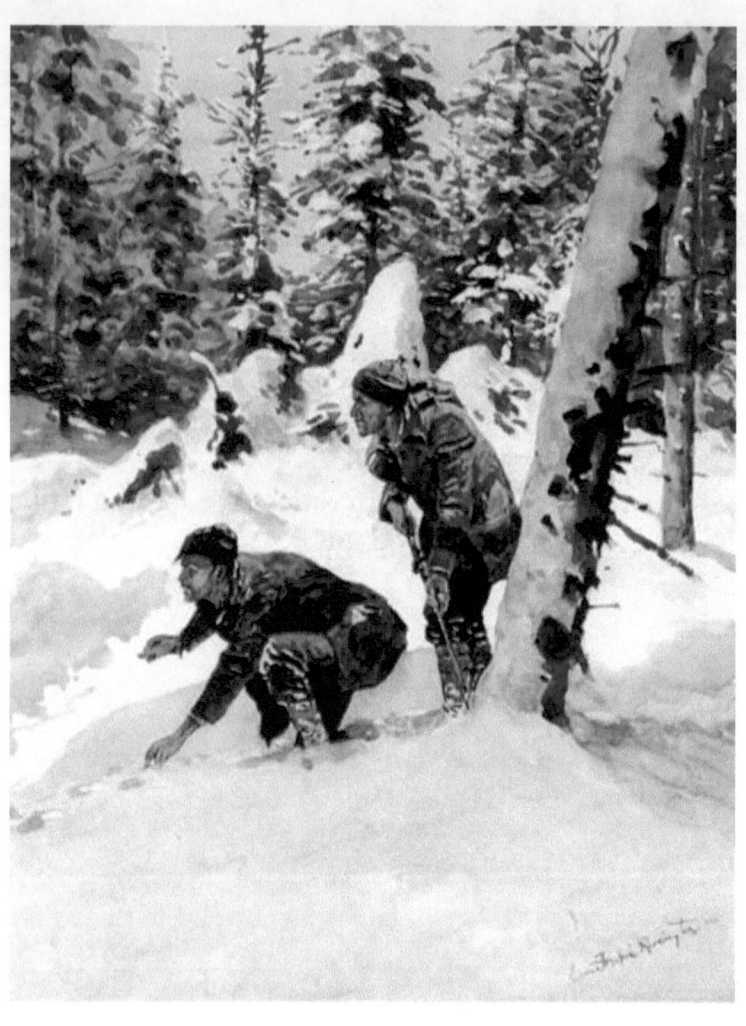

On the Caribou Tracks, 1898, Ink wash on paper

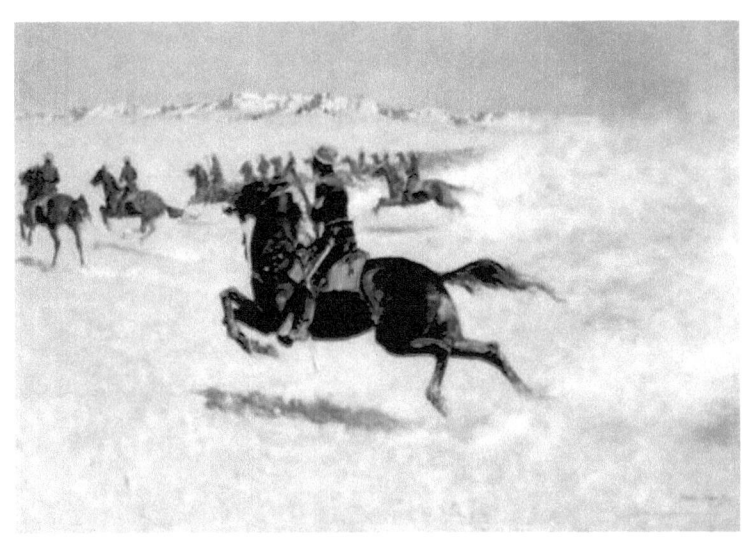

The Pursuit, 1898, oil

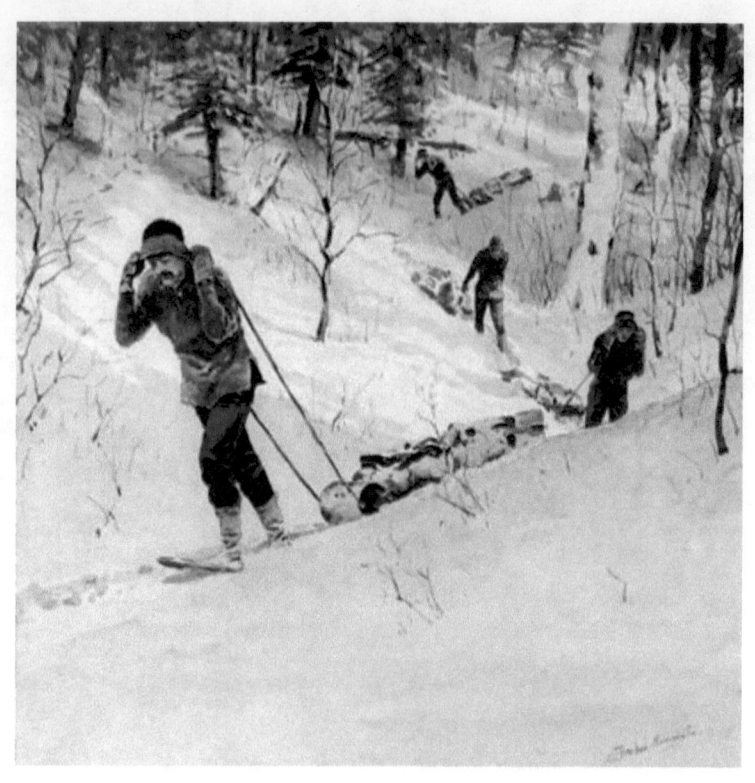

The White Forest, 1898, Ink wash on paper

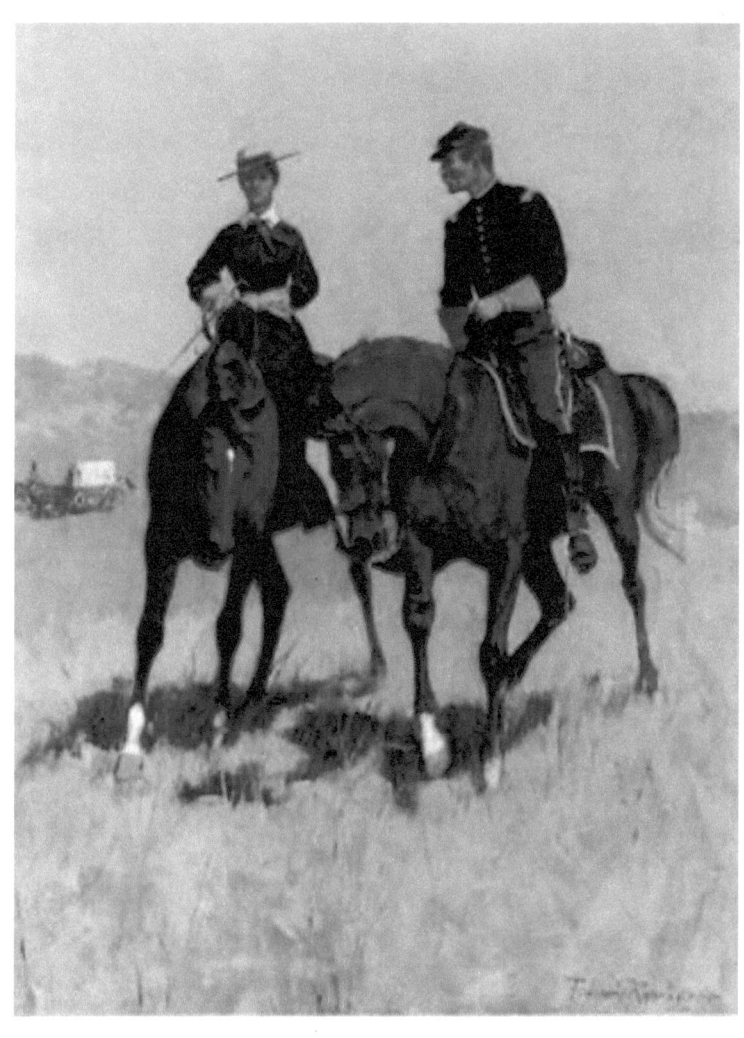

Belle McKeever and Lt. Edgar Wheelock, 1899,
oil

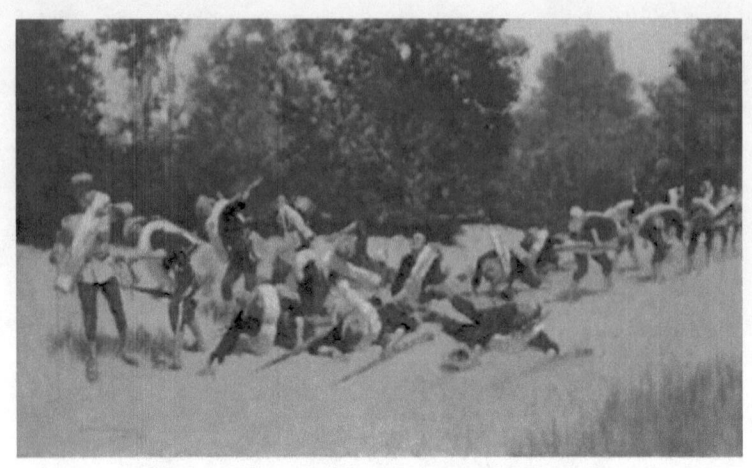

The Scream of Shrapnel at San Juan Hill, 1898, oil

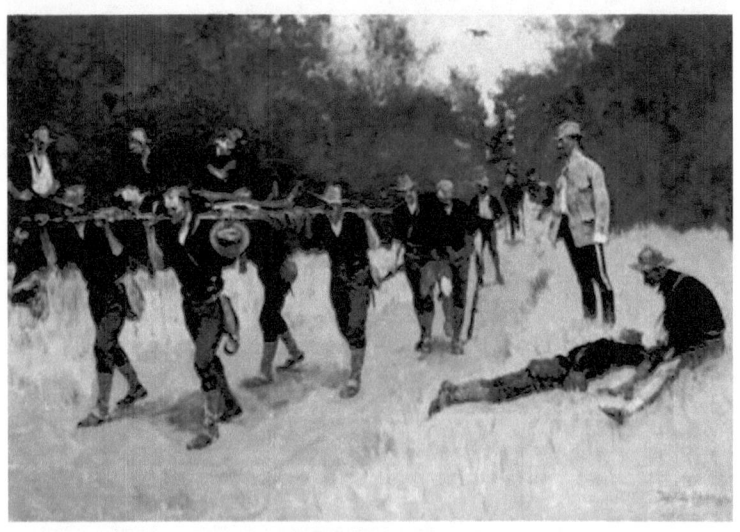

In the Rear of the Battle: Wounded on the San Juan Road, 1899, oil

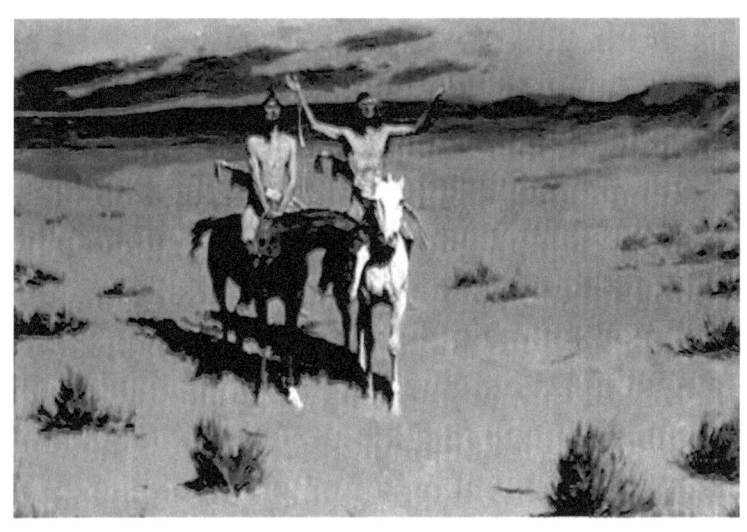

Pretty Mother of the Night—White Otter is No Longer a Boy, 1900

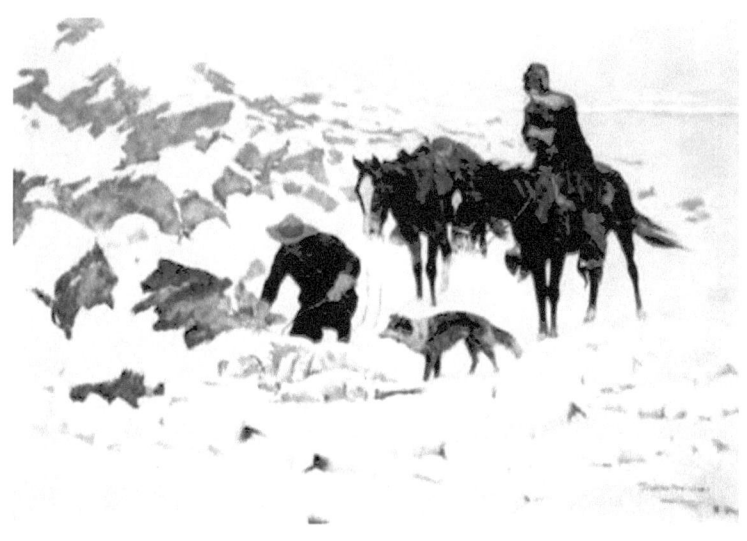

The Frozen Sheepherder (also known as The Last Watch), 1900

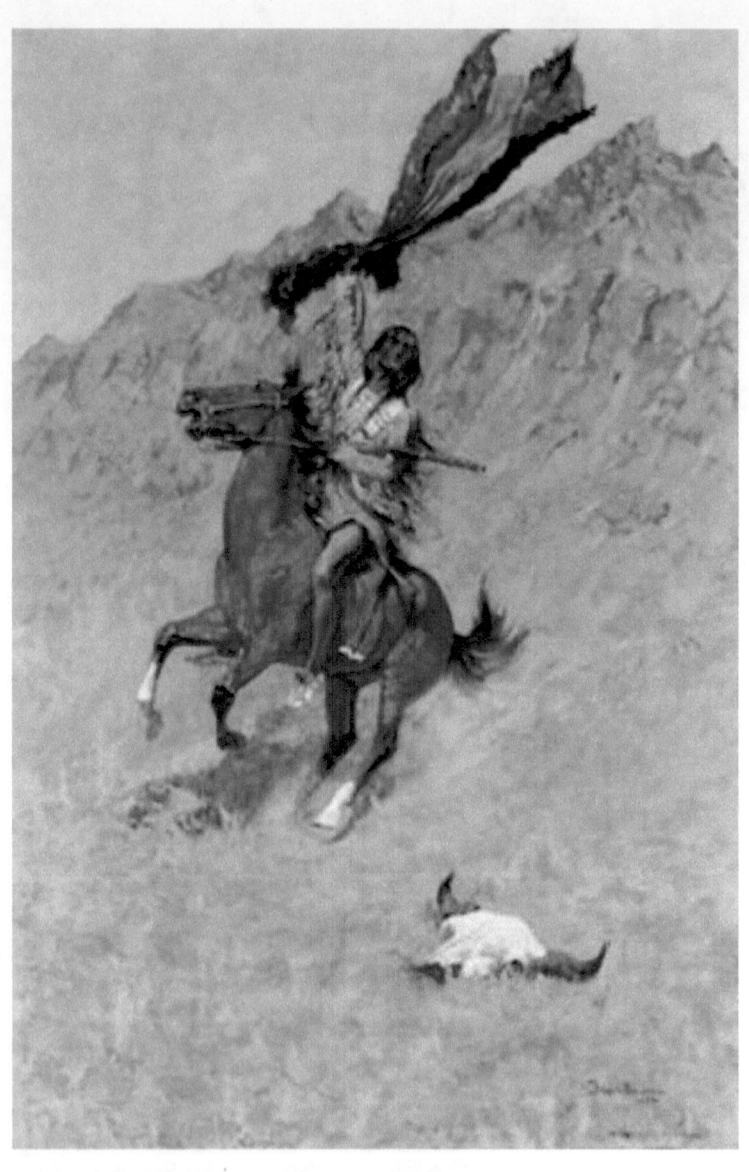

The Signal (also known as If Skulls Could
Speak), 1900

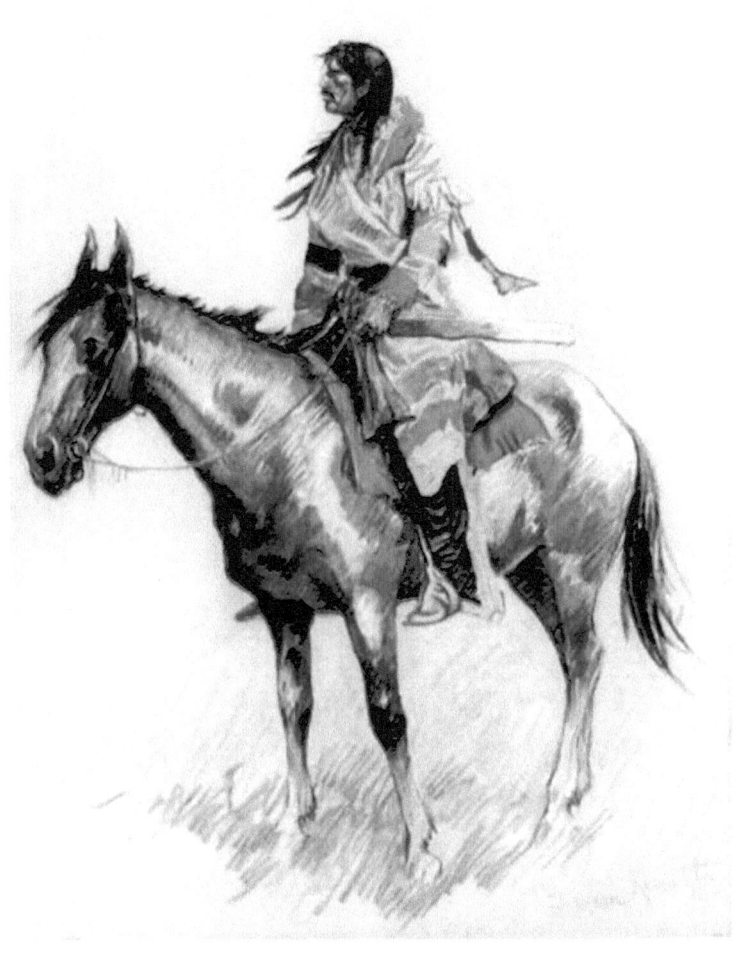

A Breed, 1901, pastel

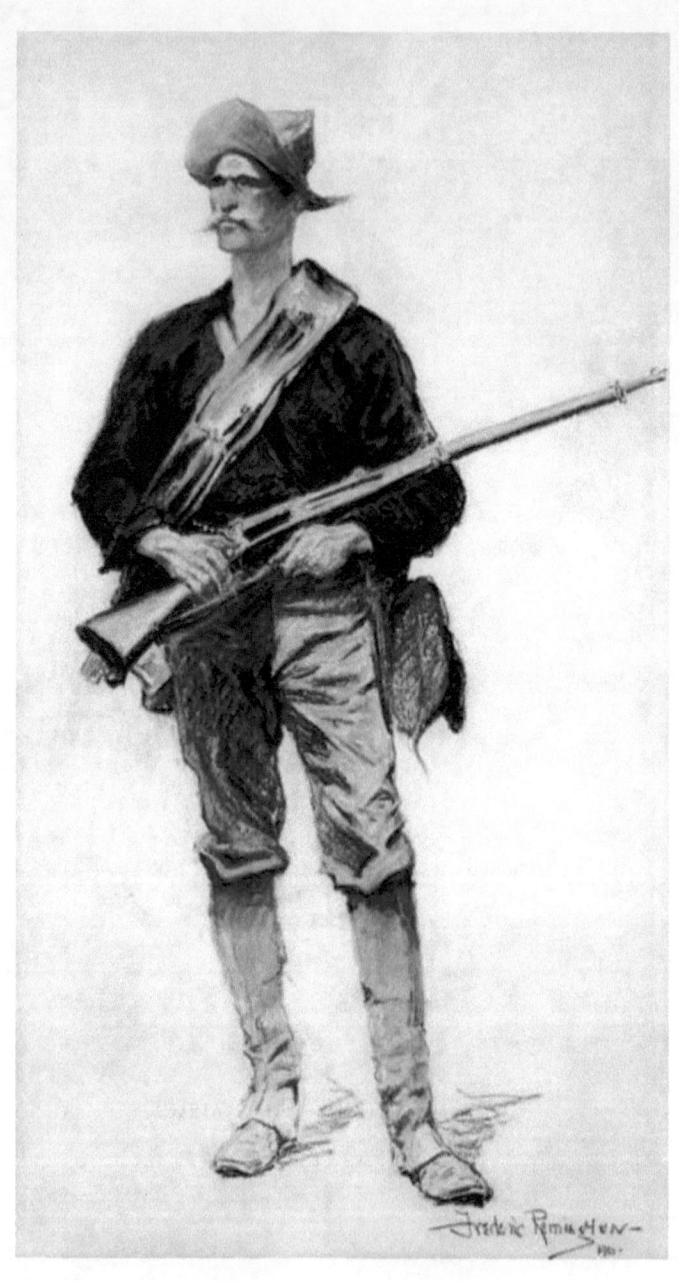

Infantry Soldier, 1901, pastel

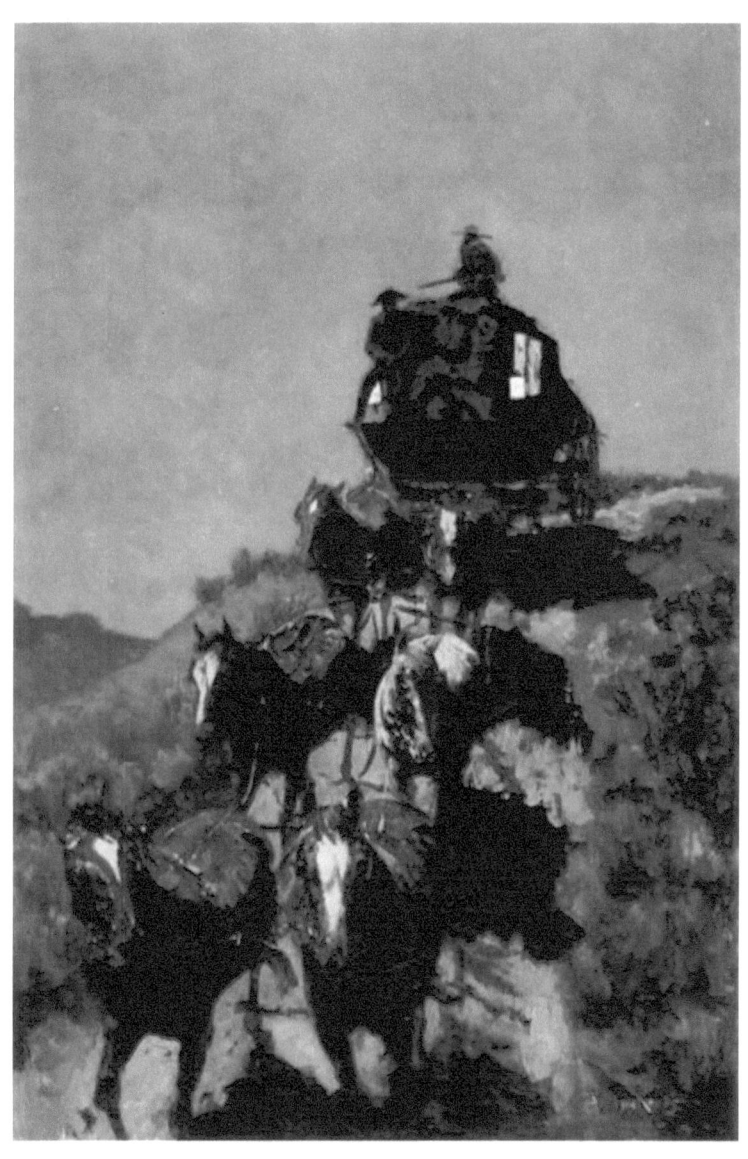

The Old Stage Coach of the Plains, 1901, oil

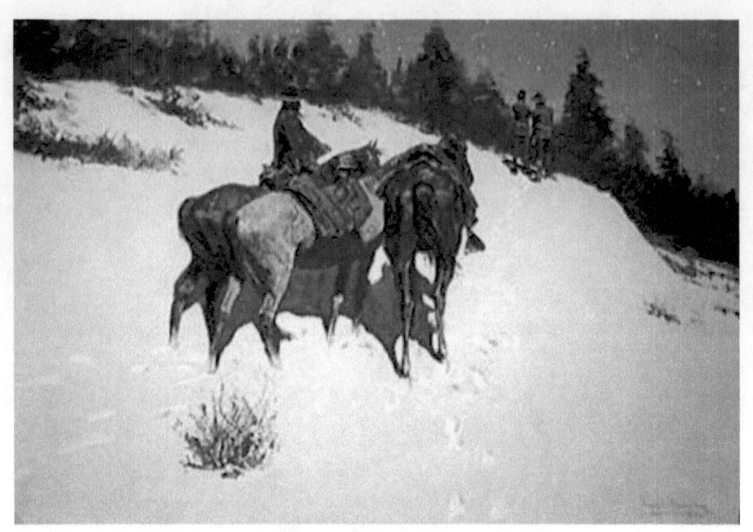

A Reconnaissance, 1902, oil

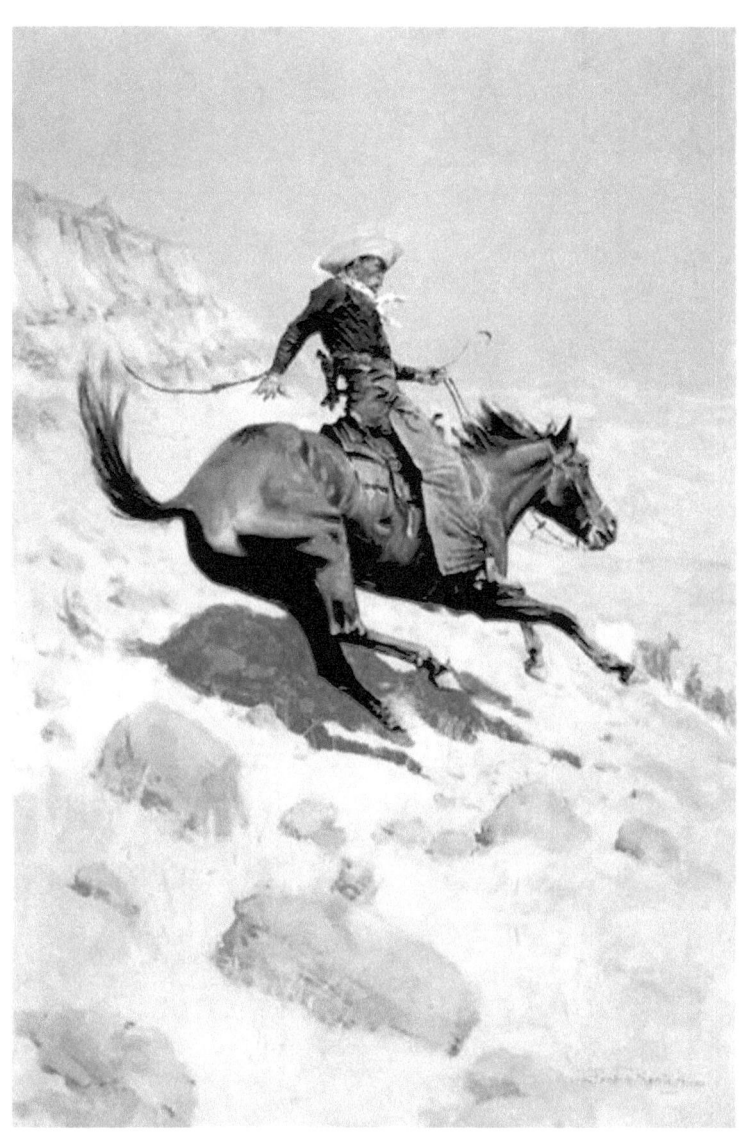

The Cowboy, 1902, 1902

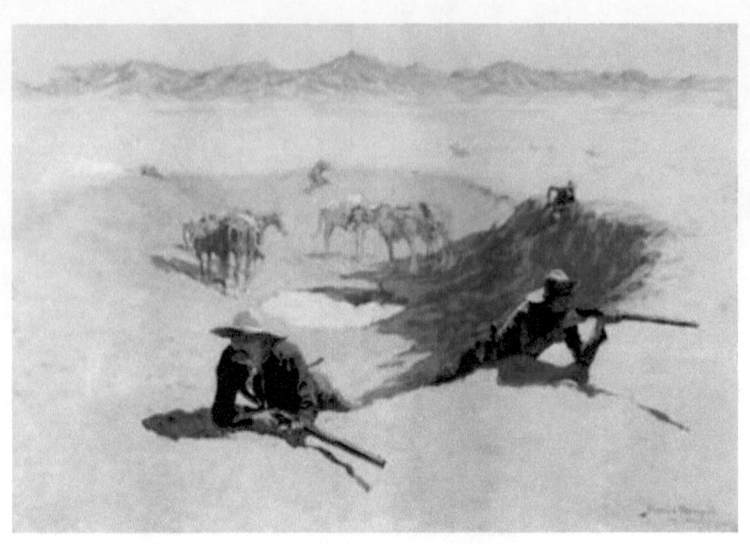

Fight for the Water Hole, 1903

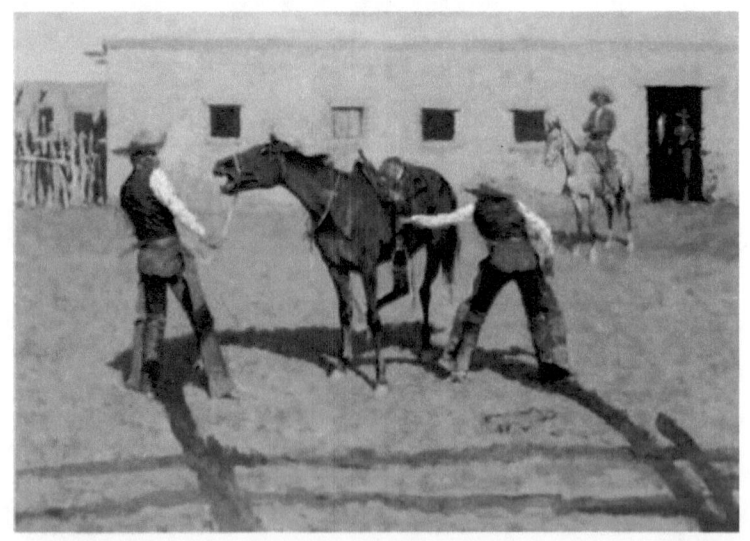

His First Lesson, 1903

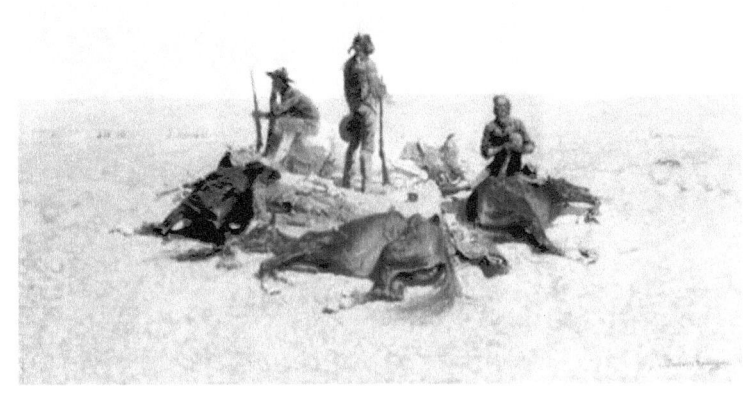

The Last Lull in the Fight (also known as The Last Stand), 1903

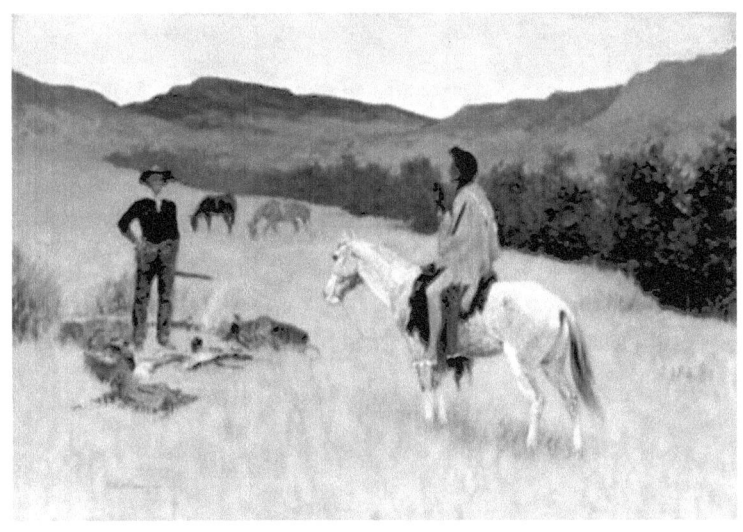

The Parley, 1903, oil

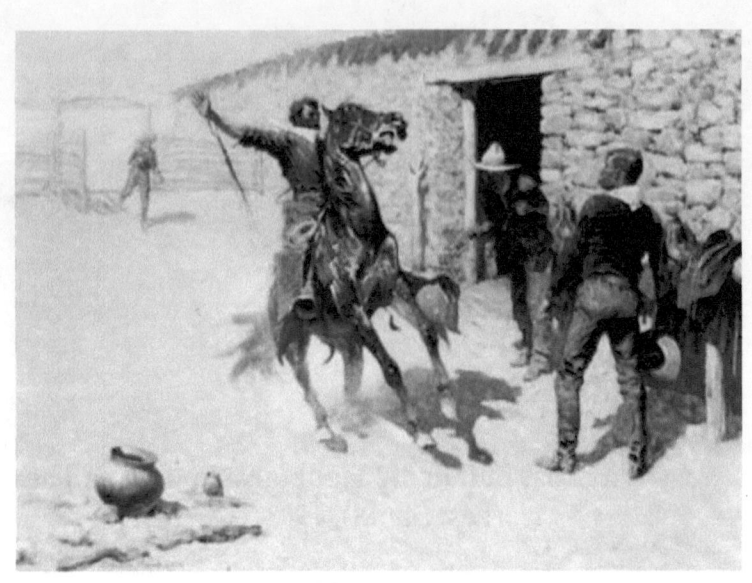

The Apaches!, 1904, oil

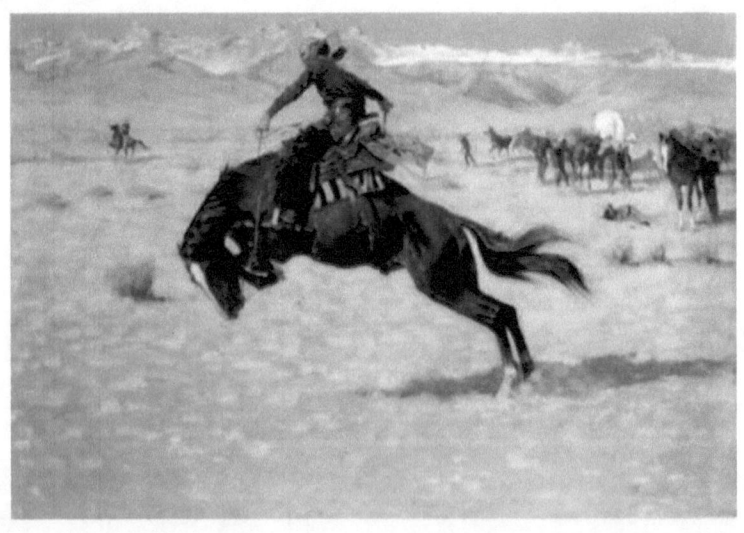

A Cold Morning on the Range, 1904, oil

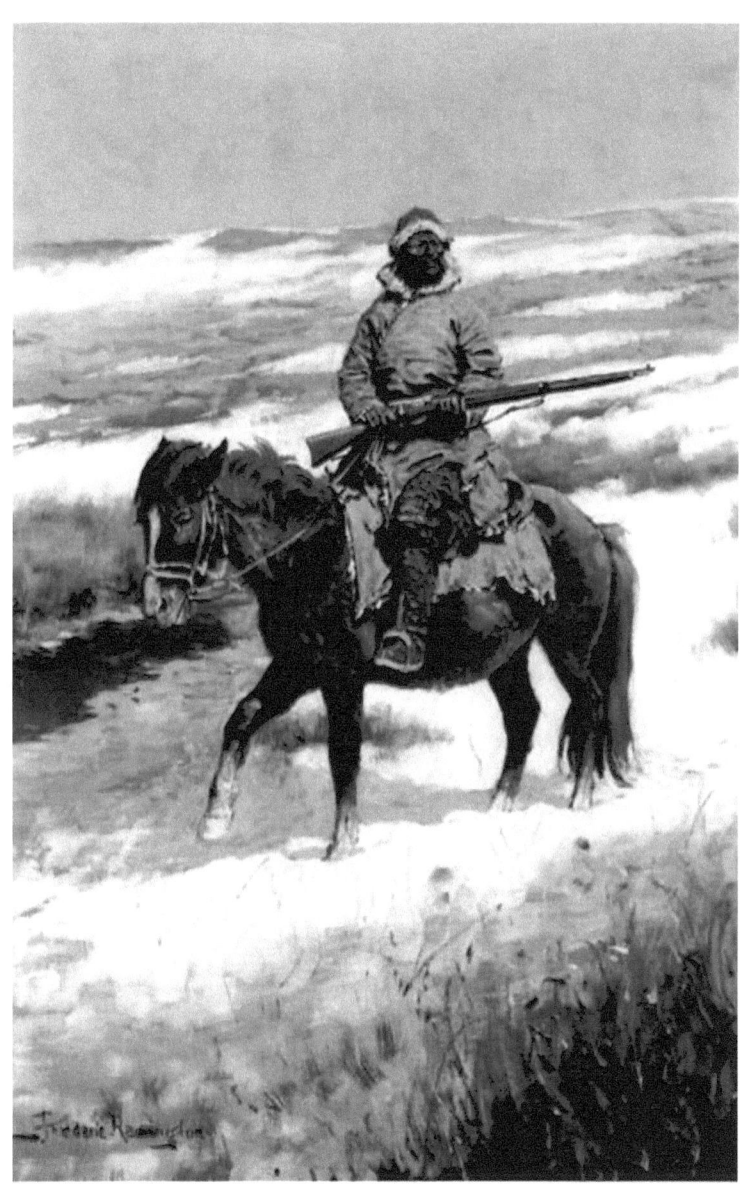

A Manchurian Bandit, 1904, oil

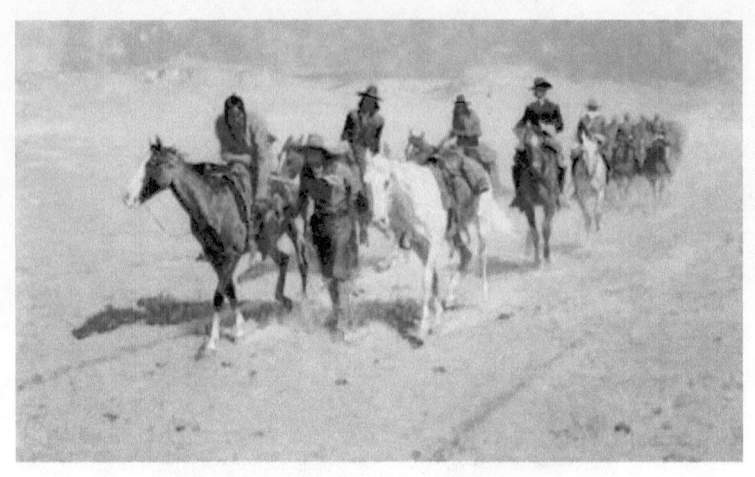

Pony Tracks in the Buffalo Trails, 1904, oil

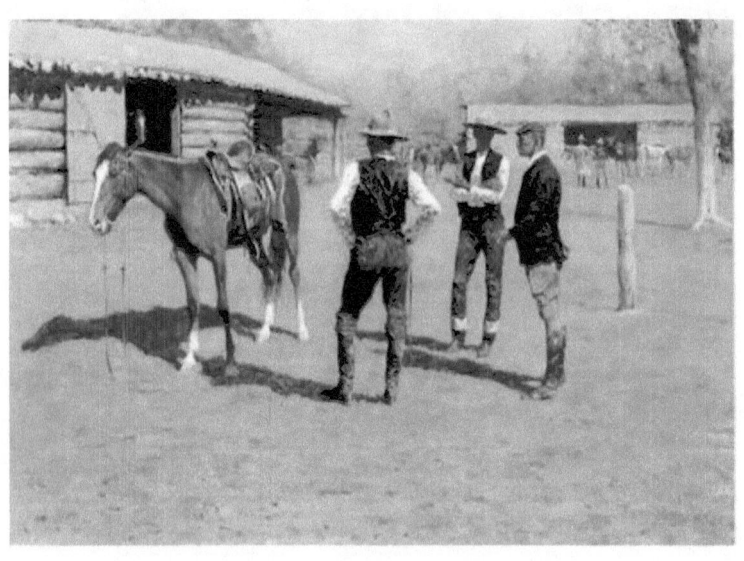

Buying Polo Ponies in the West, 1905, oil

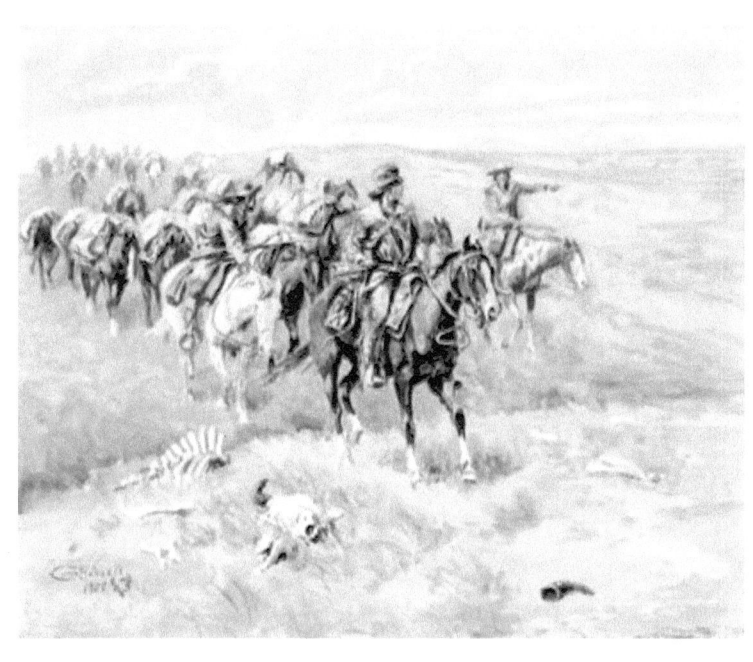

The First Trappers, 1905, gouache

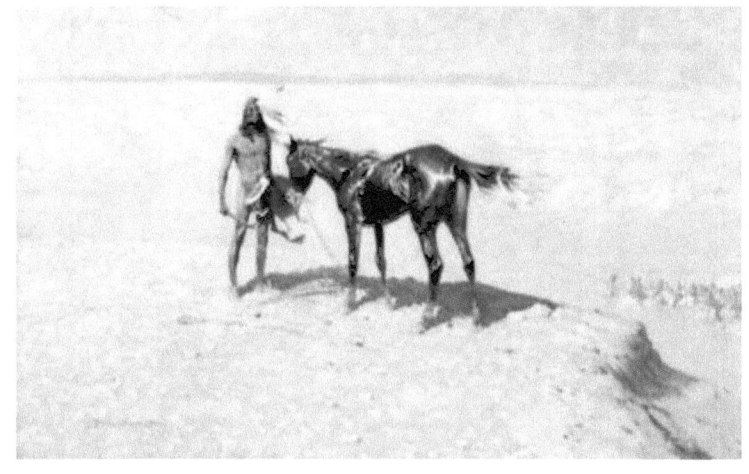

Ridden Down, 1905, oil

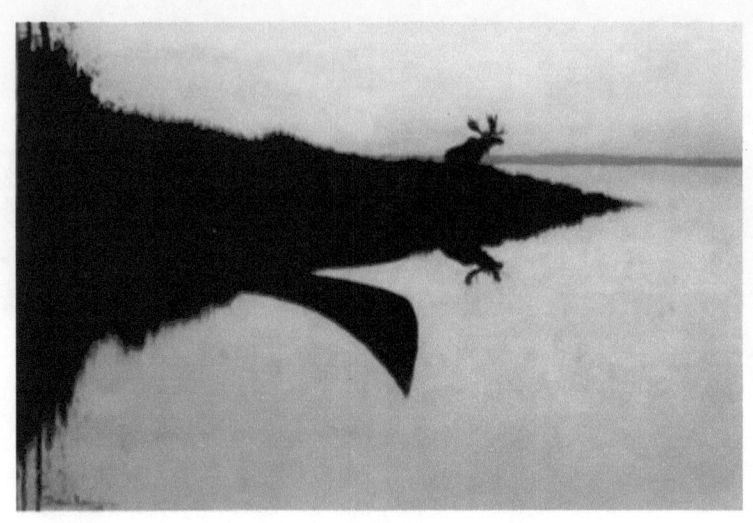

Coming to the Call, 1905, oil

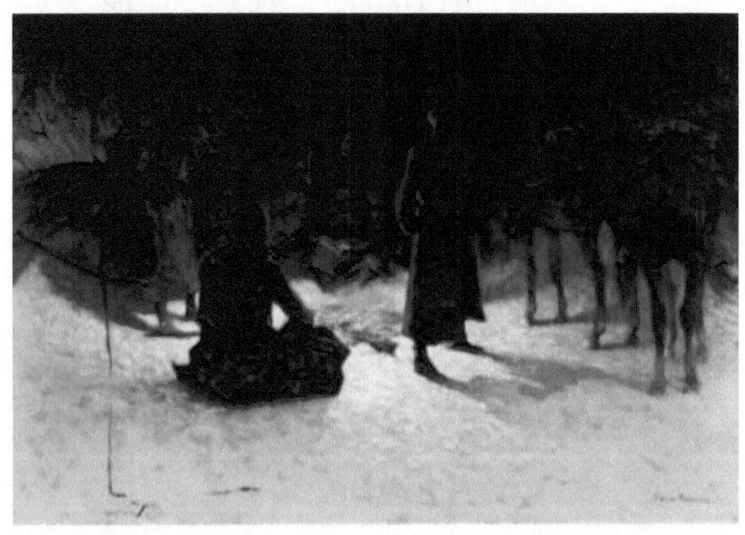

A Halt in the Wilderness (also known as Halt of
a Cavalry Parol to Warm), 1905, oil

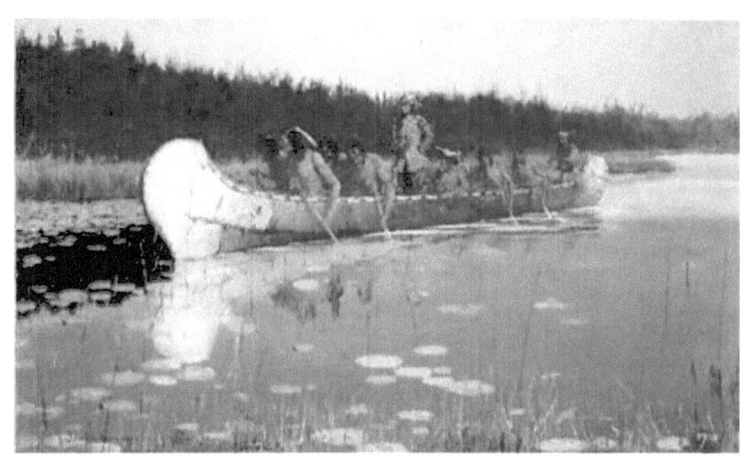

Radisson and Groseilliers, 1905, oil

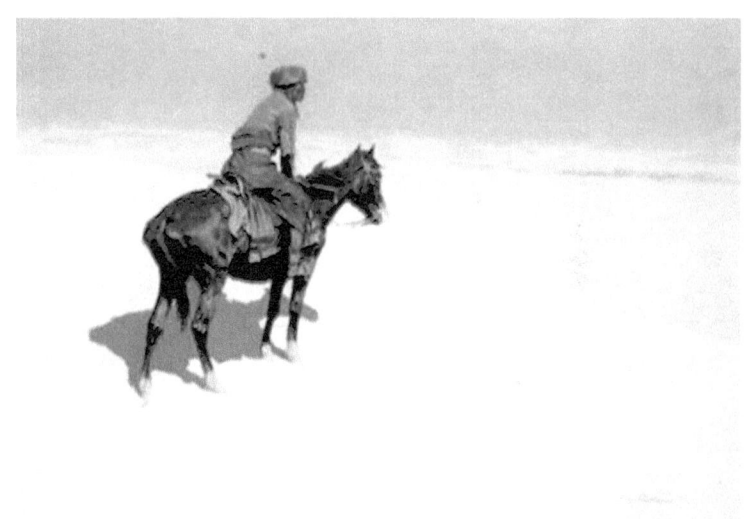

The Scout: Friends or Foes?, 1905, oil

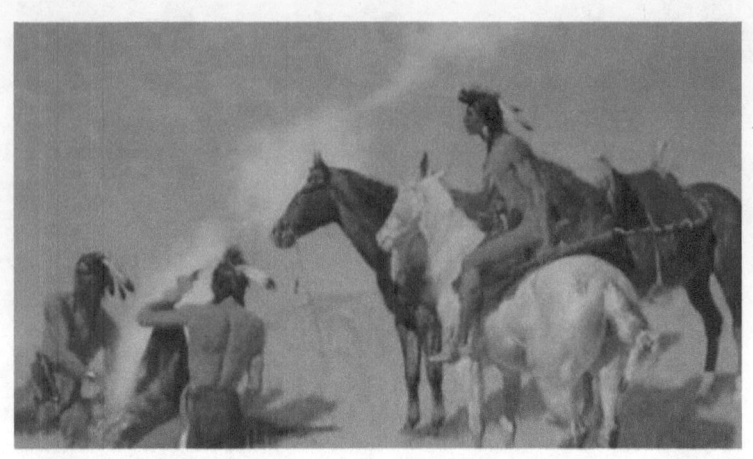

The Smoke Signal, 1905, oil

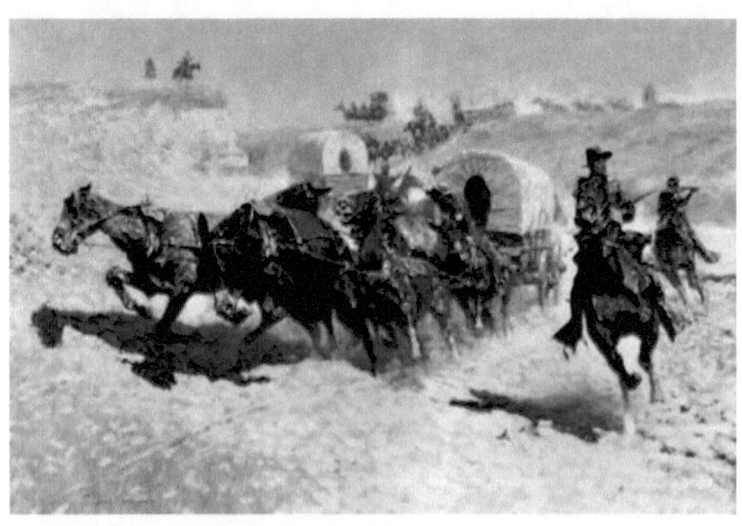

Attack on the Supply Wagons, 1905, oil

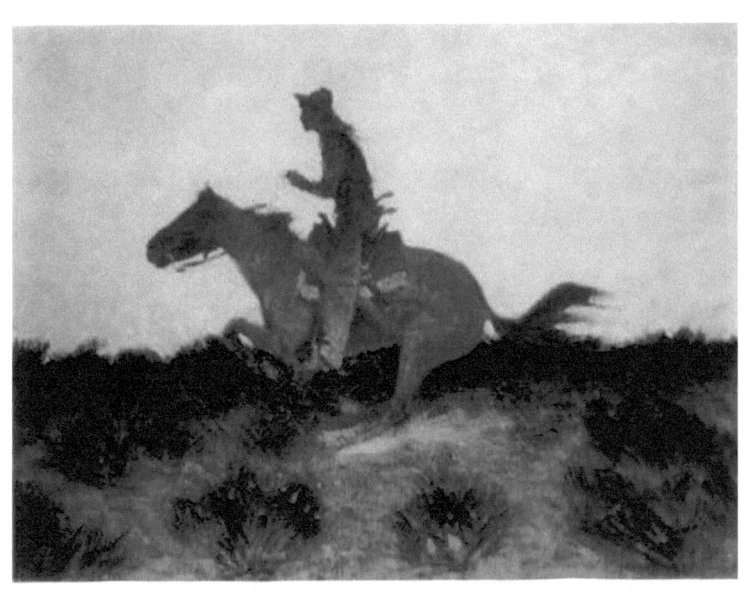

Against the Sunset, 1906, oil

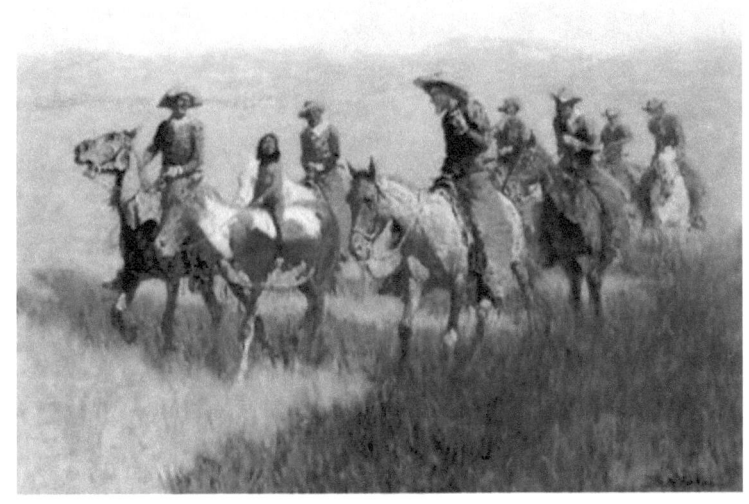

An Assault on His Dignity, 1906, oil

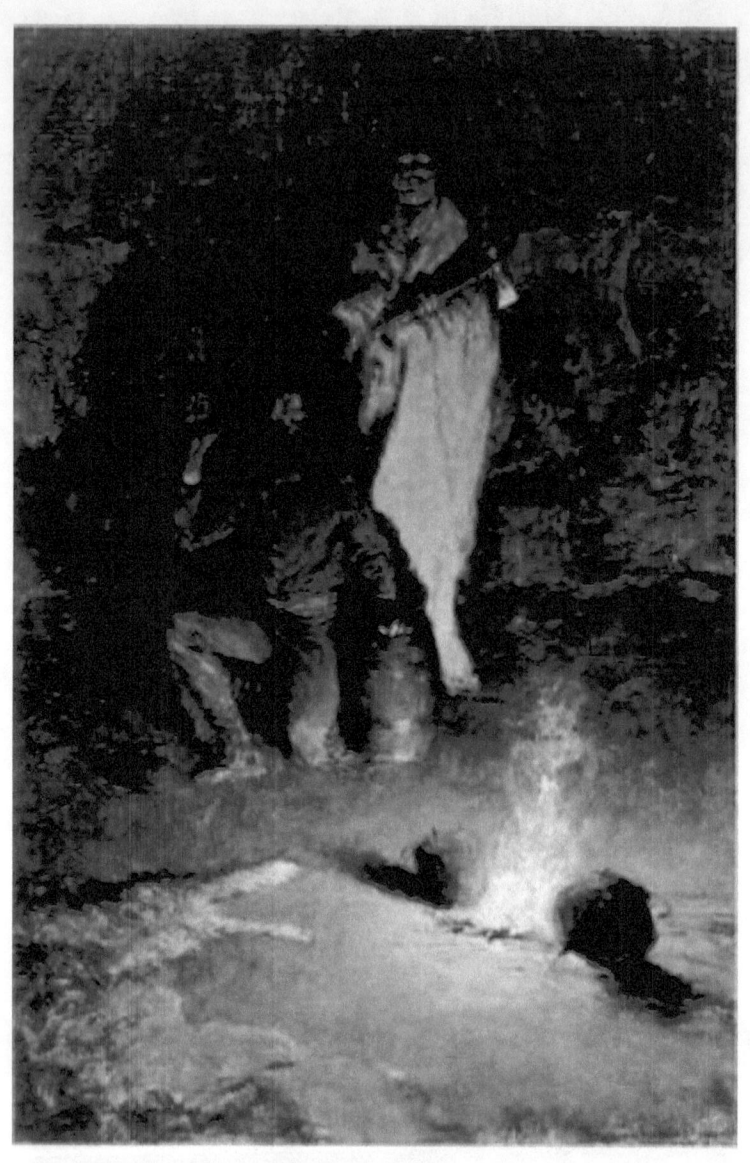

Guard of the Whiskey Trader, 1906, oil

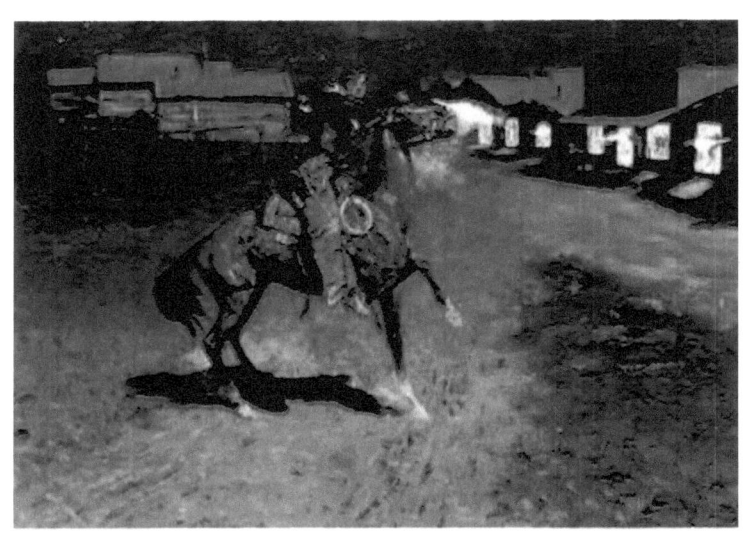

An Arguement with the Town Marshall, 1907, oil

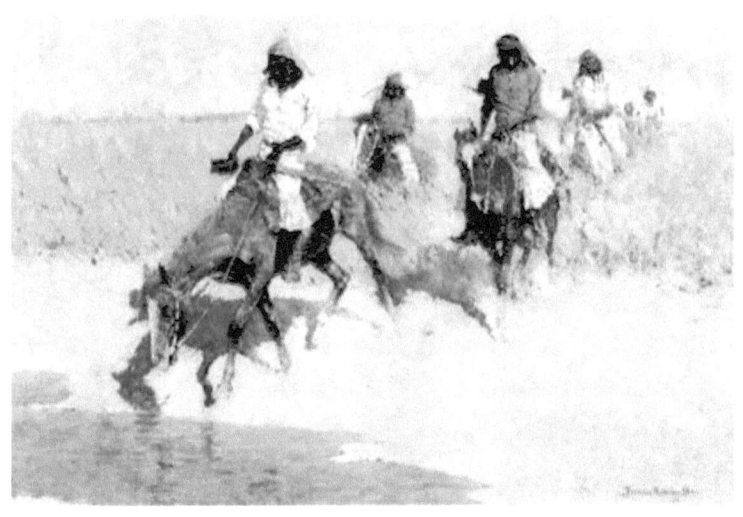

Pool in the Desert, 1907, oil

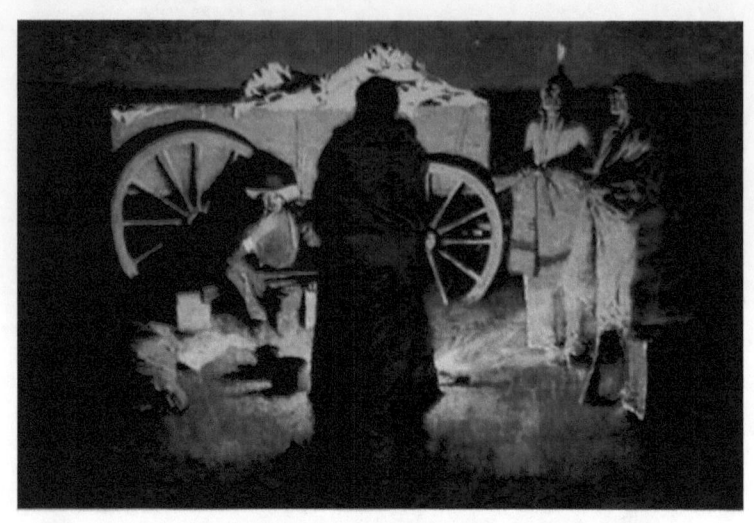

Shotgun Hospitality, 1908, oil

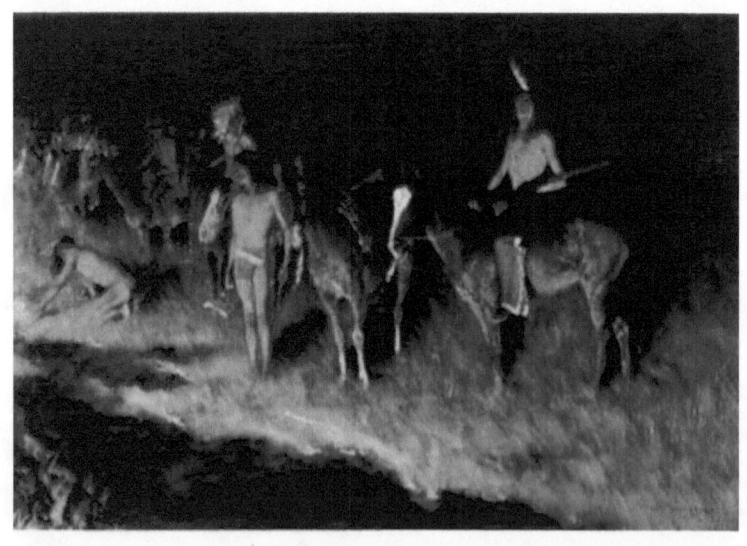

The Grass Fire, 1908, oil

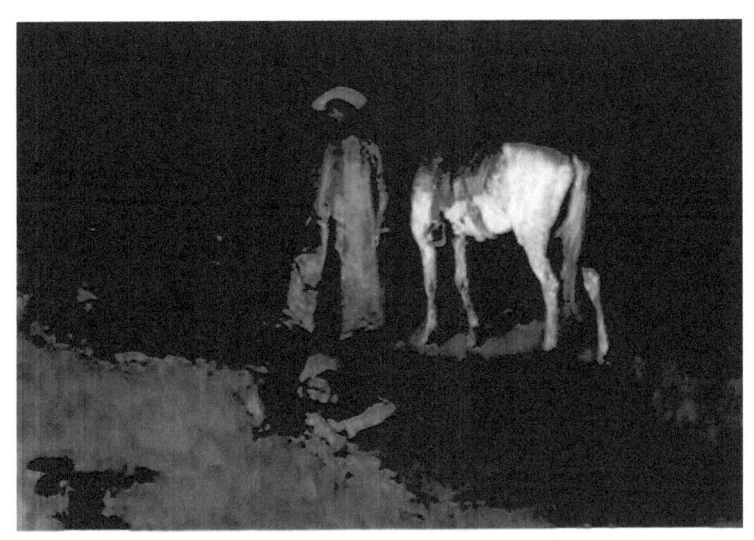

In from the Night Herd, 1908, oil

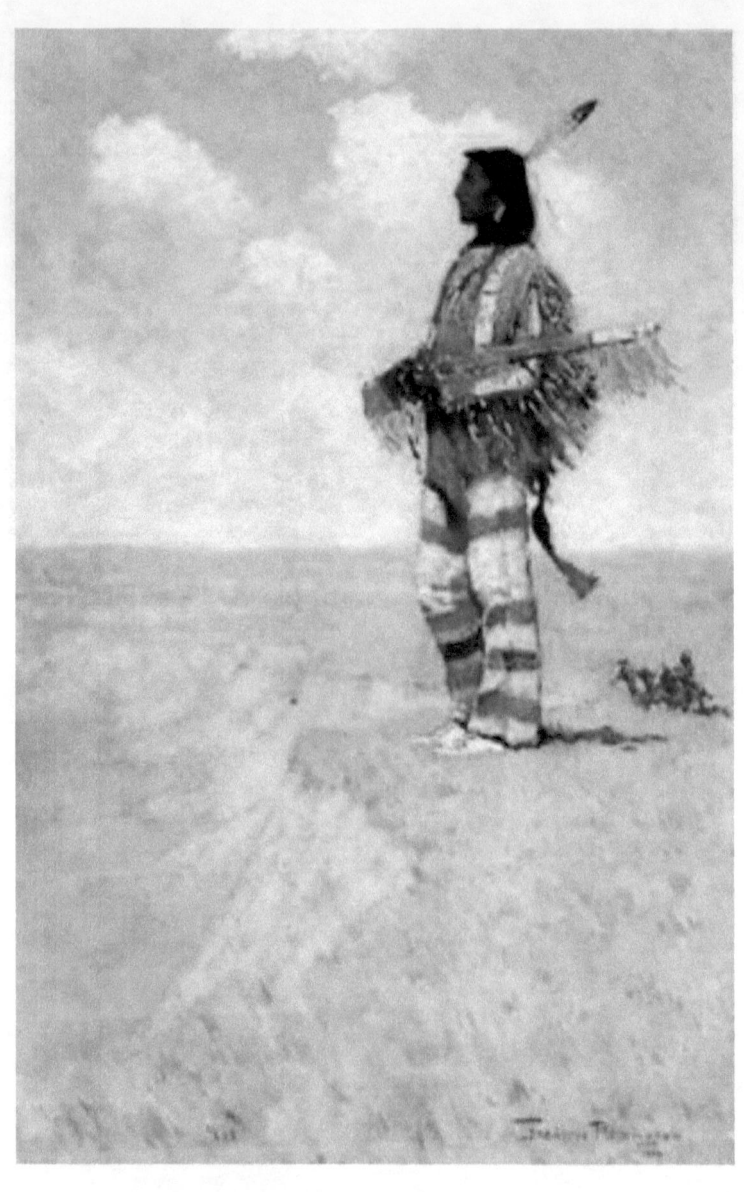

The Last of His Race (also known as Vanishing
American), 1908, oil

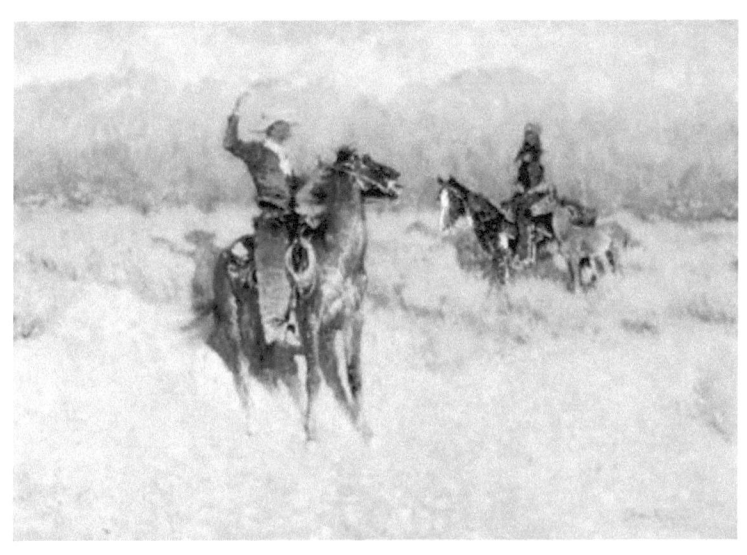

The Long-Horn Cattle Sign, 1908, oil

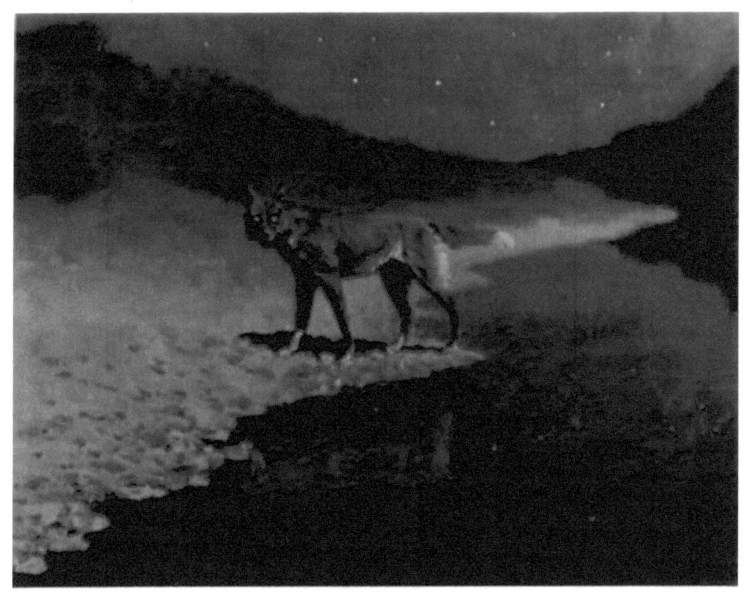

Moonlight, Wolf, 1909, oil

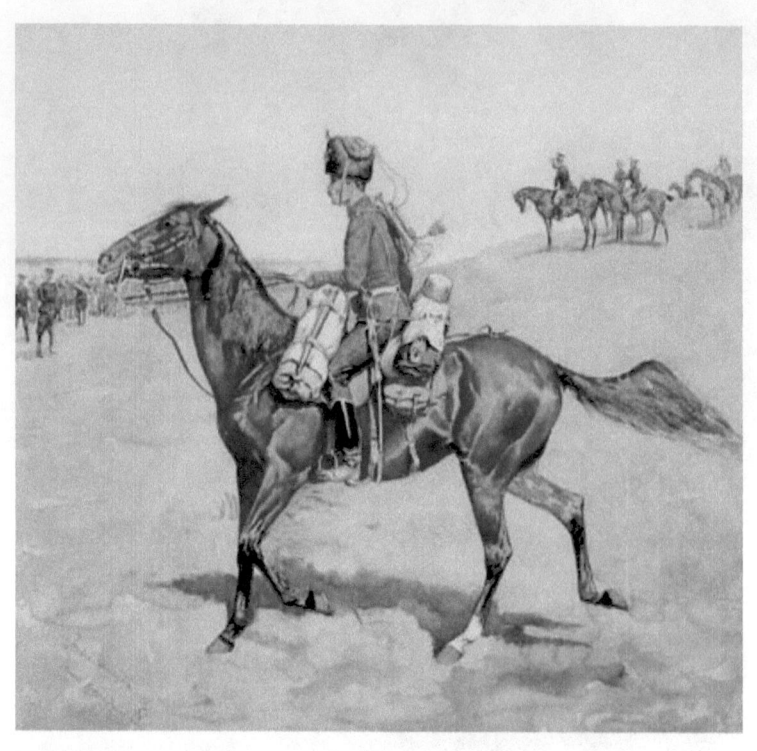

Hussar, Russian Guard Corps, watercolor

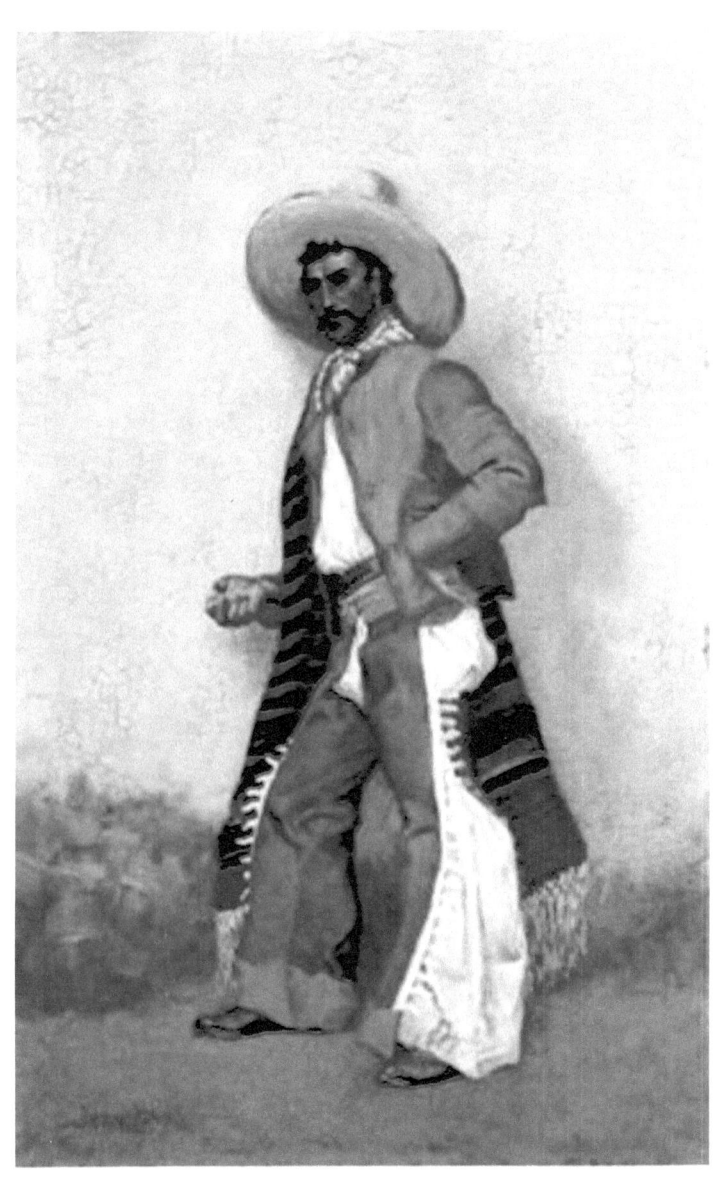

A Vaquero, oil

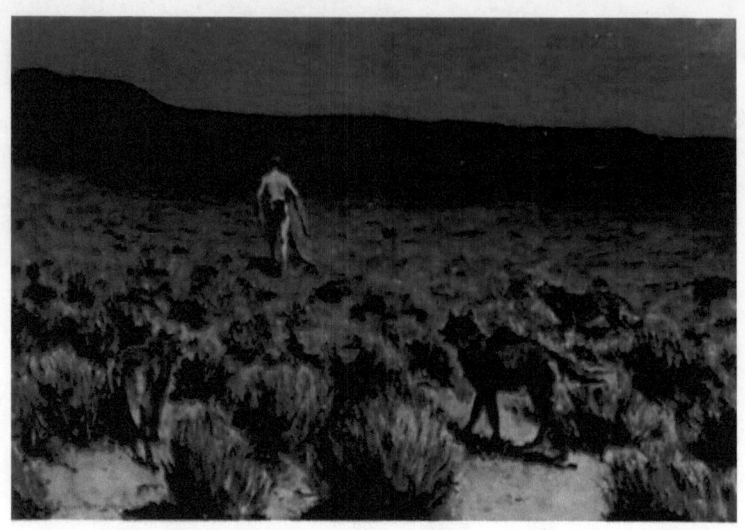

The Wolves Sniffed Along on the Trail, but
Came No Closer, oil

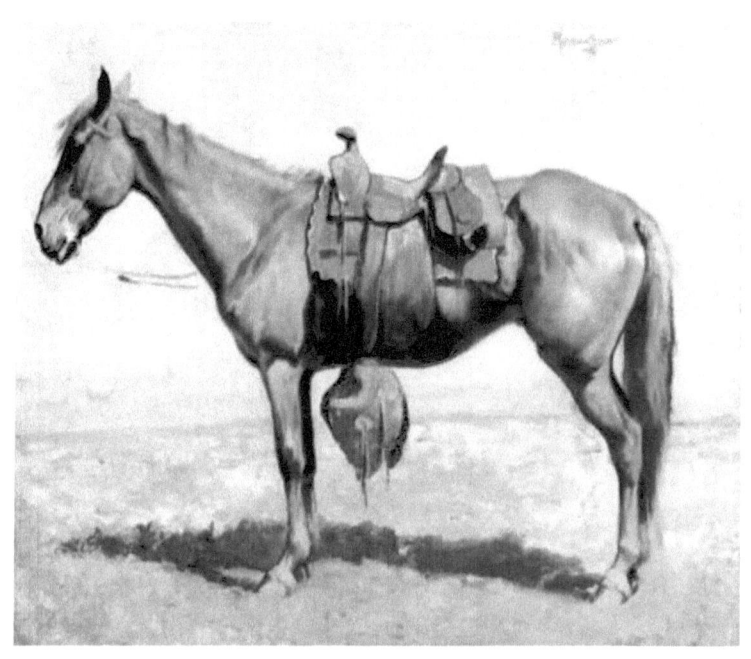

Cow Pony, oil

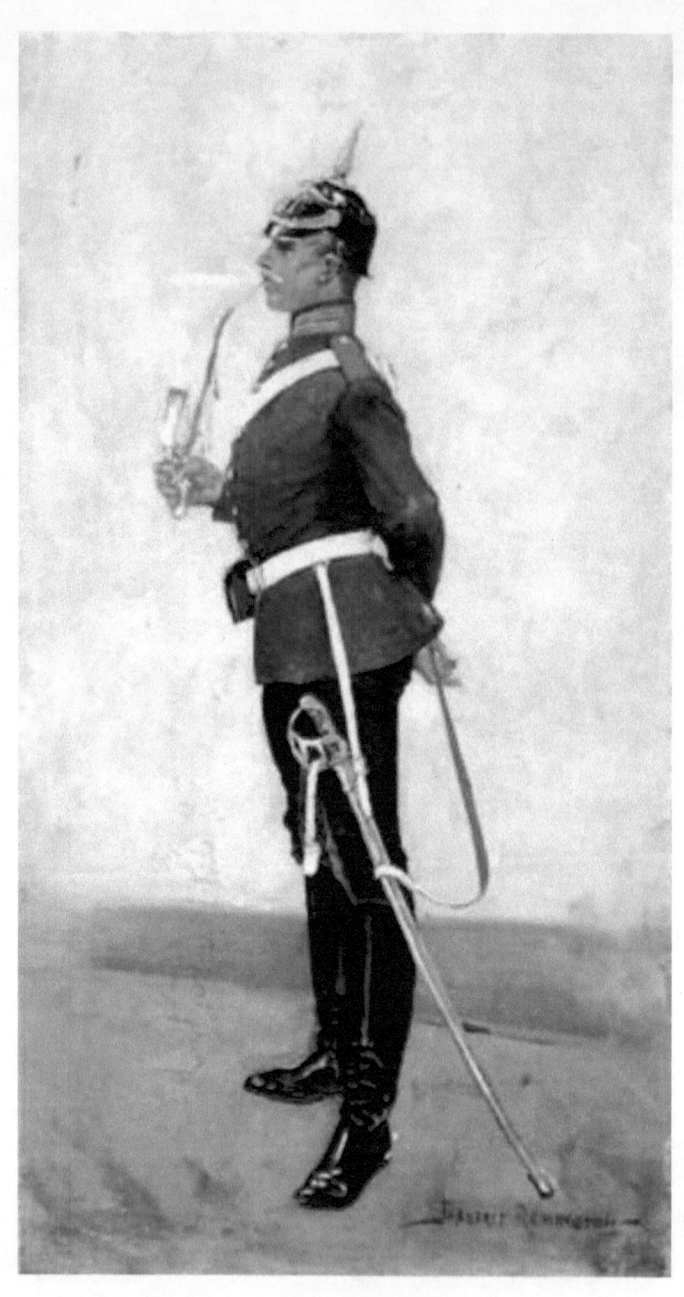

Infantry Officer, Full Dress, oil

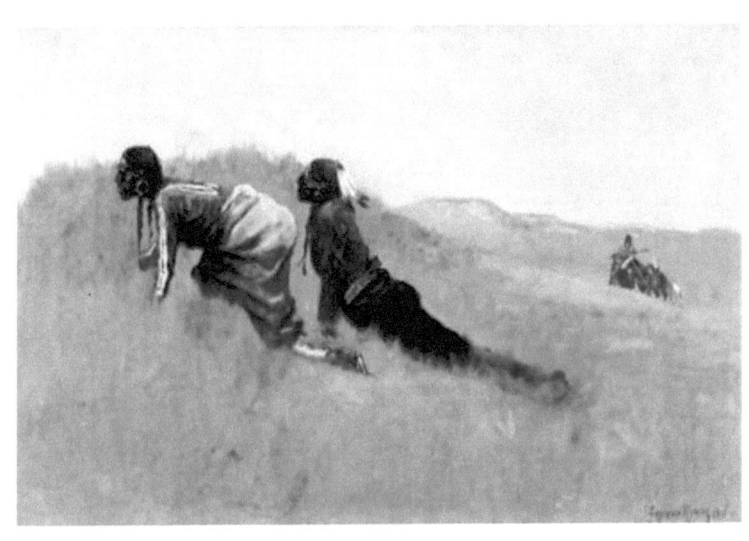

Indian Scouts Watching Custer's Advance, oil

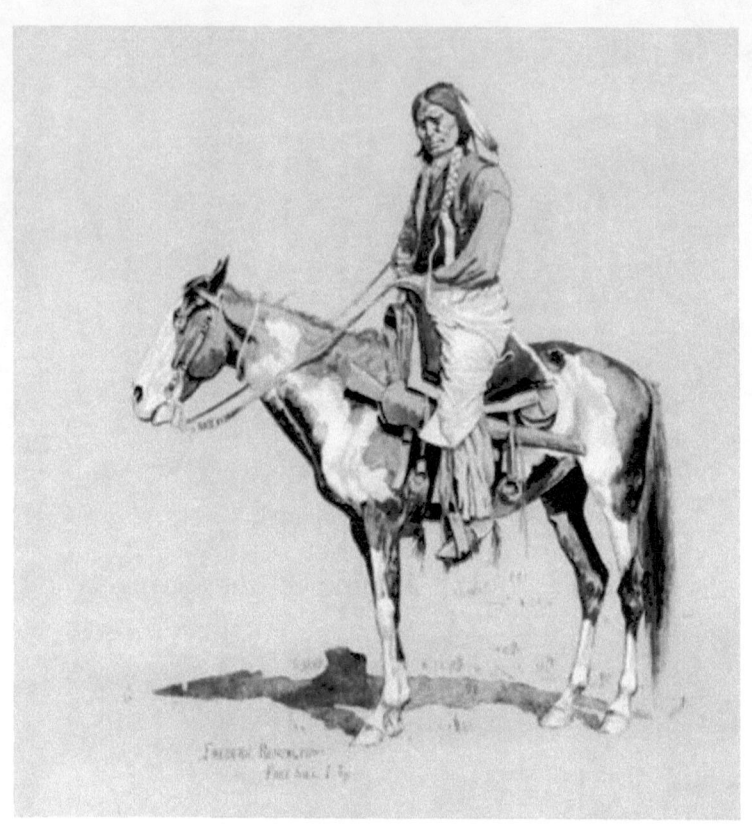

Commanche on Horseback, nk, guache and
wash on paper

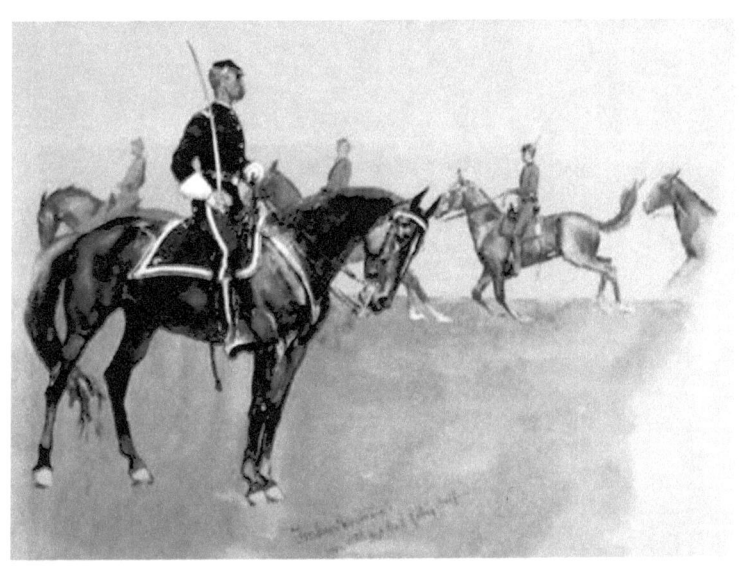

West Pont Riding Hall, watercolor and gouache
on board

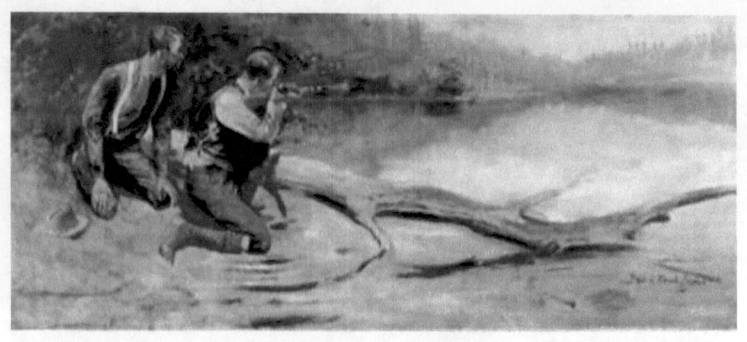

The Winchester, oil